CLIO MEDICA

# MEDICINE AMONG
# THE AMERICAN INDIANS

BY
ERIC STONE, M.D.
Providence, R. I.

WITH 17 ILLUSTRATIONS

HAFNER PUBLISHING COMPANY
NEW YORK
1962

Reprint Edition
by arrangement
1962



Published by
HAFNER PUBLISHING COMPANY, INC.
New York 3, N. Y.



Library of Congress Catalog Number: 62-17511



First Edition 1932
Paul B. Hoeber, Inc.

*Printed in the U.S.A.*
———
NOBLE OFFSET PRINTERS, INC.
NEW YORK 3, N.Y.

Fig. 1. Swallowing the Great Plumed Arrows, climax of the Mountain Chant; a medical ceremony of the Navajo. In border are the symbols found in the sand paintings used in the ceremony. (From painting by the Author.)

# EDITOR'S PREFACE

This little volume is one of a series of handbooks which under the general title of "Clio Medica" aims at presenting in a concise and readable form a number of special phases of the long and complex history that underlies the great edifice of modern medical science.

Since the times of the Aldines and Elzevirs, small easily portable booklets have been popular with the intelligent reader. Today books that add no appreciable burden to the coat pocket are real helps to the busy worker or student in gaining ready access to considerable worth-while reading. Such booklets, too, seem peculiarly appropriate for a new line of approach to such a subject as the History of Medicine from a different point of view than has hitherto maintained. From the very nature of this subject, when treated in a general way, it has thus far appeared either in ponderous tomes or, if in smaller volumes, in such scanty garb that almost no details of the costume are discernible. Then, too, the strictly chronological method of approach, with emphasis on prominent individuals, becomes almost a necessary form of treatment in the comprehensive general histories. The searcher for knowledge of the history of some small branch of the subject—a specialty, say, or the progress of medicine in this or that country—is thus forced to hunt, often painfully with help of index and marker, through the pages of the larger book or books, to be rewarded with a necessarily disconnected and usually incomplete presentation.

Our hope is that the series "Clio Medica" will obviate these difficulties. Conveniently small and inexpensive, yet prepared by recognized authorities in their chosen field, each volume will aim to present the story of some individualized phase of the history of medicine in such compact, connected, convincing and reasonably complete form that the medical undergraduate, the specialist, the busy general practitioner and the "intelligent layman" will all be attracted to a few hours' reading, which in many cases will doubtless prove the introduction of an awakened interest to a more comprehensive study.

An increasing interest has recently become manifest in the history of medicine in the English speaking as well as in other countries, as is shown by the successful formation of new societies, journals and institutes for the study of the subject. The times, then, seem auspicious for this venture. Several volumes of the series are already in course of preparation; as these materialize more will be undertaken with the possibility of a large number being attained. We bespeak the support of our colleagues and friends and pray that the Goddess whose name we have used to designate our series may deign to foster the undertaking!

E. B. KRUMBHAAR.

PHILADELPHIA, PA.

# AUTHOR'S PREFACE

My brother and I spent the long Sunday afternoons, at a certain period in our boyhood, in the tobacco reeking "den" of my paternal grandfather. He was a benign old gentleman with a pleasant chuckle, a wooden leg and a gift as a raconteur. These all fascinated our boyish fancies and we would sit spellbound hour after hour, listening to rambling tales of the Plains, the Rockies and the Pacific Coast; for the old gentleman had been an officer in constant active service in the regular army from 1860 to 1898. His memory lingered most fondly with his years of "Indian fighting"; from 1868 until the middle '90s he had been in the West, for the most part, on the Plains. Fort McKinley and the Big Horn Mountains, the early years of Fort Smelling, winter after winter in one company camps in Arizona or Colorado; Boise, Walla-walla, are the names and places I recall. The result of this doting listening was a hodge-podge of misunderstanding and misinformation about the American Indians; the general ideas being concentrated in the belief that the Indian was a rather exalted and unusually sporty game animal, with the open season holding all year round. This also seemed to be the prevalent idea of the other boys and probably is a chief reason that for generations so many disastrous mistakes were made and are still being made in our relations with the Indians.

But a more or less accidental visit to the Field Museum in Chicago wiped out at one blow my easy and superficial conception of the American

Indian.   My first view, in the museum cabinets,
of the design, color and craftmanship displayed
in the quill, bead and feather ornamentation of
garments, was a revelation which has only been
exceeded by a more recent knowledge of the mythology of the American Indian. Here was obviously a culture of which I had never heard and at
a high level that I had never been led to suspect.
The museum also showed some group models of
certain Pawnee medical ceremonies. On procur-
ing a descriptive brochure, a wealth of imagery,
symbolism and pageantry was discovered that
can hardly be surpassed by any culture. A dip
into the tales of pioneers, voyagers, explorers and
missionaries revealed not only occasional scraps
of medical lore but strange bits of fascinating
ceremony.   Further search brought to light many
short articles by medical men who came in contact
with the Indians; in many cases published in long
discontinued medical journals; and finally un-
earthed the wealth of material compiled by the
ethnologists of the Bureau of American Ethnology,
the Heye Foundation and a dozen other sources
of scientific study of Indian culture.

However, the material on the medical practices
of the Indians, while voluminous in the aggregate,
is hidden in short fragments under a mountain of
other lore. Finding nowhere a volume in which
this was gathered under one cover, I determined
to assemble this in one place for more ready refer-
ence by any who might become interested in the
matter. Of necessity, a great deal of data has had
to be omitted; therefore an extensive bibliography
has been included in this volume.

My thanks are due to Mr. Hoeber, the editor of this series, and the staff of the Museum of the American Indian (the Heye Foundation), for encouragement, helpful suggestions and aid in finding references.

ERIC STONE

Providence, R. I.
April, 1932

# CONTENTS

# CONTENTS

# LIST OF ILLUSTRATIONS

CLIO MEDICA

# MEDICINE AMONG THE AMERICAN INDIANS

## CHAPTER I

## THEORY OF MEDICAL PRACTICES

### RELIGION AND MEDICINE

THE practice of medicine among the Indians of the United States area prior to their contact with Europeans cannot be understood without some knowledge of their spiritual life and religious beliefs. Their mythology and theology are peculiarly rich and endowed with an unexpected symbolism and beauty, bespeaking an unusual ability to express their emotional and esthetic appreciation of their all important physical environment. Their metier was not pictorial, but lay, on the one hand, in decorative design and on the other in a wealth of folklore and poetry. For instance, most of the songs of the Pawnee "Hako Ceremony," can scarcely be surpassed in lyric quality by the best of European poetry. Or again, there is a delicacy and a yearning for beauty in certain songs of the Navajo "Mountain Chant" that seem strangely at odds with the traditional picture of the Indian as a brutish savage.

One of the favorite pastimes of the Indians of all
sections of the country was the telling of tales and
legends. Each club or society, each family and
tribe and class had its own particular myths, told
and retold through centuries and rivalling in
ideation and detail the myths of the Greeks or
Scandinavians. We are most familiar with a tale
of a Minnesota tribe reproduced by Longfellow in
his "Hiawatha." The journey of the Hero-God in
the myth of origin of the Menomini "Mitawin"
is as colorful as the Greek "Odessey." It would tax
a Diaghilev to reproduce scenically the word
pictures of the dwellings of the gods visited by the
semi-divine originator of the Mountain Chant.
The recounting of these folk tales was elevated to a
fine art and night after night in thousands of tepees
and lodges the Indian story teller perfected his art
in perpetuating the colorful traditions of his tribe.

Nor are these the expression of certain gifted
poets; the understanding of nature, the appreciation of the beauty and the perfection of existence
were intimately woven into the daily life of each
individual Indian. Throughout life he walked hand
in hand with his deities. His every act was watched
over by some supernatural agent. Every design,
the shape and adornment of every implement, the
presence of every feather or quill symbolized some
appropriate religious concept. While the Indian
never worshipped the article or image, and was in
no sense an idolater, yet he symbolized in even his
simplest possessions some spiritual quality. Where
a spoon or a bowl is dedicated to a deity, when the
entry into a tepee involves an obeisance to the god
presiding at the hearth, when the sowing of seeds
demands an elaborate ceremony; it is not surpris-

ing to find that the medical practice is deeply tinged with mysticism and ceremony.

All forms of religion among the Indians were essentially uniform in character, and although many of the deities and the terminology varied greatly, yet ceremonies were identical in tribes that were ethnologically quite dissimilar. The Medicine Dance was performed from the upper half of the Mississippi to the Hudson Bay, from the foothills of the Rockies to the Hudson River, being practiced alike by the central Algonkian, the Siouan tribes, the Plains Cree and the Ojibwa.

The uniformity of the various religions was a polytheism based on nature worship. The myths of origin of the secret societies of widely separated tribes are peculiarly alike, despite wide variations as to the cultural level of the tribes; and all take their roots in the personification and deification of the creatures and elements of earth and sky. With some tribes there was hardly a theology despite their elaborate ceremonies, while contiguous tribes had well-developed religious tenets. The formal theology of the Skidi Pawnee was, perhaps, the most highly developed of all, both as to ritual and belief. It sounds strangely familiar to one conversant with other primitive pagan theologies, Egyptian, Greek, Roman, African and Malaysian. In the Pawnee Pantheon Terawa, the creator, ruled supreme; and to him the lesser gods and all animals and human beings owed allegiance. His spouse, the Vault of Heaven, stood next in the hierarchy. Then came the Evening Star, who, through her relation with the male principle, the Morning Star, became the mother of the first

human being, incidentally a woman. Next in
importance were the four cardinal points of the
compass. Through the fifth group, Wind, Cloud,
Lightning and Thunder, Terawa made his ordi-
nances manifest to the lesser earth gods and to
man. The earth gods were more intimately asso-
ciated with the people than the others. They
included the various animals, fish, birds, plants,
lakes, mountains, etc. Each individual, each
family, each class, each village revered its own
particular earth god. The members of the tribe
were even divided into social groups dependent
on the earth god inherited or selected by the
individual.

This multiplicity of supernatural agents was
believed to influence not only the more important
crises of life but every act of the daily routine.
Therefore, it was only natural that the Indian
attributed the inexplicable ailments that beset
mankind to the anger of the gods or the malevolence of the more evil of the spirits. This is not
peculiar to the American Indian. The development of European medicine is inextricably
commingled with European demonology, theology
and philosophy. The Egyptian priest was the
practitioner of the healing arts, the early Greek
philosophers were the pioneers of medicine, the
African and Malaysian shamans were the doctors,
as were the Scandinavian priests. In all these
groups physical ills were believed to be due to
some slight to, or to the malevolence of, some one
of the multitude of the deities that controlled life
at every point. The cure of disease was supposed
to be achieved by the mollification of the offended
or offending god, and protection against disease

was attained by propitiation of the entire hierarchy of celestial beings.

The theologico-physical dualism of the American Indian is best illustrated by his use of the word
"Medicine." To the person brought up in the
European tradition, medicine connotes some
chemical, some regime of life or physical procedure
used for its actual alterative effect on the body.
To the Indian the term means much more. He
may use the word to refer to an herb or drug, but
more often it means some supernatural article or
agency which may be of aid in curing disease or
just as often the same thing may be invoked to
insure the success of some individual or tribal
undertaking. Anything under the sun might
achieve such therapeutic or mystical quality,
might become "medicine." Once invoked, the
article thus dignified was held to be powerful and
sacred. It might be an animal, a bit of wood, a
finger from a powerful foe, a spear or a pipe. But
once consecrated, it was never harmed if animal,
or never again used for lay purposes if it were a
utensil. This did not mean that the article was
revered in itself as the Indian was always careful
to distinguish the fact that its symbolism alone
hallowed it. These articles or herbs or even formu-
lae which were supposed to have healing or other
benign properties were spoken of as "good
medicine," while evil influences or things were
referred to as "bad medicine."

The Indian boy of almost every tribe, before
achieving manhood, was expected to retire to some
secluded spot, a lone mountain peak, some desolate
depth of the forest, or an arid plain, and "make
his medicine." There he fasted, prayed, mortified

his flesh and meditated until he had worked himself into a religious fervor, exactly similar to that of the early Christian ascetics in their cells. This state predisposed him to dreams and visions. In this auto-suggestive ecstasy he was sure to receive some communication from the gods; the appearance of some animal or bird, some unusual conjunction of the elements, or some fantasy which would reveal to him the supernatural agent guarding and directing his life. This would become his "medicine" and would in the future be invoked in times of social, mental or physical stress. Or the method of determining one's guardian might be such as that employed by the Pawnee. Among this tribe, when a child fell ill, medicine-men were called in and the supernatural agent called forth by the medicine-man who effected the cure was understood to be the fetish presiding over that child's destinies.

Thus it is obvious that "medicine" to the Indian was not only physical but spiritual; and was brought into play not only to cure disease but to advise, protect and insure success in both the ordinary and the unusual events of life of the individual, the family and the tribe. While realizing that many of the practices used by the Indian in his treatment of disease were also used in influencing the course of social and civic events, we will in this paper refer only to their use in association with the sick.

# CHAPTER II

## MEDICINE-MEN AND MEDICINE SOCIETIES

The medicine-men were important in the social organization of the tribe and were either chiefs or if not were ranked next to the chiefs. They were to be found among all races and tribes of the Amerinds, although their relative numbers and formal organization varied greatly from tribe to tribe. In no tribe was there a priestly class and usually the rank was not hereditary. The theurgists were supposed to have supernatural powers conferred on them by the gods, especially the earth gods in animal form. Through this deputation of the occult they were possessed of four types of power. First and foremost they could cure the sick; then they had the ability to perform feats of magic (in reality clever sleight of hand tricks). Thirdly, they could subject others to their will, thus rendering the subject or patient quiescent and susceptible to the healing influences conjured up by the medicine-man. This was a sort of hypnotism and had, in the belief of the Indians, a further characteristic: it could be shot like an arrow into a person at a distance; and if the intentions of the mystic were evil, could cast the person into a spell which would lead to death. The victim was powerless unless he consulted some other medicine-man who recognized the spell and could employ some counter magic to cast it out. Fourthly, they had the power of enlisting the gods in favoring various undertakings, or could induce the gods to bring rain or insure a plentiful crop or successful raid or hunt. They could interpret the wishes of the gods through interpretation of dreams and omens.

Women as well as men could enter this select group. They might achieve their position through the appearance of some unusual vision or a communication from the gods in a dream or while in a state of ecstasy, or through the possession of a palpably psychic personality, or through some curious conjunction of circumstances. An Apache woman was considered to have become a shaman after she had miraculously survived two accidents: she was first mangled by a mountain lion and later was struck by lightning. It was natural to assume that any one who could survive such ordeals was possessed of supernatural powers. Among certain tribes admission into the circle was more formal. Among the Hopi and the Navajo certain young boys were dedicated to the medical clans. At an early age they went to live with the elders of the societies and received years of training in the dances, mysteries and ceremonies as well as the material therapeutics of their calling. But among most tribes the usual means of entry into the profession was through apprenticeship to an established practitioner. The apprentice lived with and studied under his mentor for a year or more. The process was an expensive one as the theurgists demanded exorbitant fees for such instruction. The numbers were further limited to those who sincerely believed that they possessed occult powers by the fear of punishment in the event of the death of a patient. If the patient died, the bereaved family might call the attendant's colleagues in consultation. If they decided that any measure which might have led to a happier outcome had been neglected, the offending practitioner was turned over to the relatives of the deceased for satisfaction in the form of personal violence or the payment of valuables.

The medicine-men were usually organized in one or more societies, as among the Pawnee or Zuni; or more rarely acted as individuals, as among the Apache. In addition to the secrets known to all medicine-men, but concealed from the rest of the tribe, each society had its distinctive secrets. And, furthermore, each member had his personal occult agencies of which no one knew but himself. There was no settled dogma or distinct theory of medicine, each practitioner consulting such spirits as were most amenable to his secrets and charms; but no two seemed to have called on the same influences. As to the administration of medicines and various types of treatment there was only the unanimity of opinion that might have existed among herb doctors of ancient Europe or appears among the wise old women in country districts among the whites of today. The individual diversity in the practice of medicine is well illustrated by the members of the medical society of the Apache who give the Spirit Dance. It was their most highly developed and sacred religious as well as medical rite. While the headdresses and kilts worn by the participants were uniform, yet the symbolic interpretation of the uniform was distinct for each individual.

There was one characteristic common to all medicine-men. Despite all the tricks and chicanery involved in their ministrations, they had complete faith in their practice, were immensely sincere and took great pride in their profession.

The medicine-men in all tribes assumed charge of the ceremonial feasts and dances; made nearly all the preparations for hunting or war parties; were consulted in the search for stolen property; were called on to foretell the success of various undertakings, individual or communal; were asked to invoke rain, petition the gods for fruitful crops; and conducted birth, wedding and burial rites; and healed the sick. In short, they combined the functions of councilor, prophet, priest and physician. In many of the tribes any medicine-man was competent to perform all of these activities; in others, as among the Cree and the Apache, there was a division of the work, various theurgists specializing in different phases of the mysteries.

They were remunerated in several ways, and usually became wealthy. Their pay depended on the wealth of the patient (frequently absorbing it in toto and that of his relatives in part), and was given in kind: buffalo robes, beads, parfleches of dried meat, horses, sacks of corn or strands of dried pumpkin, skins or utensils. In some of the Algonquian tribes where wampum was used as a medium of exchange, the physician received wampum as his fee.

# CHAPTER III

## EQUIPMENT OF THE MEDICINE-MEN

In no tribe did the medicine-man wear a distinctive form of dress, except when carrying out some ritual. The ceremonial dress was extremely variable depending on the symbolism required of the costume. They ran the gamut from the extremely ridiculous to the most beautiful examples of Indian artistry still extant. Many wore their ordinary costume enhanced by some charm or amulet. Others, notably members of the organized societies, wore the costume appropriate to some god celebrated by the societies' rites and used both in the ceremonies and at the bedside. Certain medicine-men had costumes limited in extent and variety only by the ingenuity and fancy of their wearer. These costumes will be described as they appear in the various rites conducted over individual patients or groups of patients in the sections of this book covering occult therapeusis.

Medicine masks were worn by some shamans and were usually those of their societies' rituals, as in the Zuni practices. (See Fig. 16.) A few wore medicine hats used in those rites and practices conducted by the wearer alone. Such a one was that owned by the Apache medicine-man, Nan-ta-do-task. It was a truncated cone of soft, tanned buckskin with a lobulated tailpiece, which fell down between the wearer's shoulders. The crown was ornamented by a few black-tipped eagle feathers, some pieces of abalone shells, bits of chalchihuitl and a snake's rattle was fastened to the central point of the top. Along the turned-up front brim were the usual triangular cloud designs. Across the front, just above the brim was the caterpillar-like figure of the god of the wind, with his lungs graphically portrayed. Above this was a figure of zigzag parallel lines in red, blue, green and yellow, representing the rainbow, from which lines descended as symbols of rain. This design was repeated above, entirely circling the crown. The major part of the back bore the image of a Kahn or chief god. To the right of this was the symbol of the morning star. In the center of the segments of the lobulated tail appeared symbols of other stars. The tail itself represented Nan-ta-do-task's special guardian spirit or "medicine," the centipede. These representative figures he called on during the rites conducted over his patients, and he used no other impedimenta. Other such caps are extant, all presenting shapes and symbols in curious combinations depending on the fertility of their makers' imagination.

Every male Indian of all the plains tribes and of many of the forest and plateau tribes had as his most precious possession a "medicine bag." They were only used incidentally in the practice of medicine, as the shaman's herbs were often carried in such bags along with his most sacred personal fetishes. But they are so frequently referred to and because of their name have caused so much confusion that it seemed wise to describe them and their use in this place. The Indian suffered almost irreparable disgrace if his medicine bag were lost or captured by the enemy. Such an accident could only be atoned for by capturing two from the enemy. The bag was a skin pouch bearing symbolic ornaments and containing magical trifles. The most beautiful and ornate were found among the Menomini. They were usually made of beautifully cured otter skins, the whole animal including skull, legs and tail being preserved. Other fur-bearing animals, also birds, snakes, frogs and turtles were sometimes used, the animal selected sometimes being the owner's guardian spirit. Whatever the animal, the legs were always bound with bead, quill or feather work and the tails decorated and lengthened by exquisite designs in the same media. Symbolically colored feathers always filled the nostrils. Among the Menomini certain contents were prescribed. The bag had to contain the cowrie or snail shells used in their shooting ceremony, the small lithosperm seeds used in the same rite, the blue paint used to decorate the face of the owner during the ceremony, a small packet of hoddentin, and the charm given the owner by his guardian spirit at the time he "made his medicine." Besides these the bag might contain any number of supernatural or actual medicines. The number and variety of a bag's contents determined its value. Each bag had its individual song or chant, used as a prayer by its owner; and each of the articles in the bag had a similar prayer or song, the bag being used on special occasions much as a rosary. One Menomini chief kept in his bag, now in the Heye Foundation Collection, sixty such magical articles, the bag being known as a "sixty-song bag" and therefore was of unusual value.

From the point of view of comparative medicine, the rhombus or "bull-roarer" or "whizzer" is of considerable interest. That used by the Walapi,

Pueblo Zuni, Navajo and Utes is identical in form and application with that employed by the ancient Greeks and Peruvians and by the aboriginal New Zealand and African tribes of today. The implement was a thin piece of wood about 7 or 8 in. long. There are three forms in existence: a narrow parallelogram, a narrow triangle and an isosceles triangle. They were preferably made of wood from a tree which had been struck by lightning. They were carved in symbolic designs. One of the Apache rhombi is typical of the class. It is a parallelogram ending in a round knob to which the cord was attached. This circular head was carved in the effigy of a "Kahn's" head, from which waving lines streamed down either border, giving the central part a lobulated form. These lines represent the Kahn's intestines. In each lobe is a figure representing his lungs, and also symbolizing the wind god. On the reverse are engraved many long, wavy but parallel lines, each tinted a different color, and denoting both the hair of the god, and lightning. The wood was fastened to a horse-hair or leather thong, 5 or 6 ft. long. When whirled rapidly above the head the rhombus produced a roaring sound faithfully imitating a gust of rain-ladened wind. It was employed for the invocation of wind, rain, and crops, and to cure the sick.

Medical necklaces of several kinds and remarkable forms were used; but they were rare. The famous bear-claw necklaces were not endowed with healing powers, being insignia of military rank and prowess. The most potent medicine necklaces were made of human fingers. One specimen of this unusual and macabre device is now a museum piece and is at present in a perfect state of preservation despite the fact that the embalming was done over a hundred years ago. Its major symbolism depends upon eight forefingers from the left hands of enemy warriors killed in battle by the maker, High Wolf, a Cheyenne medicine-man and warrior. They hang from a buckskin collar, and between them are hung five medicine arrowheads (which had attained supernatural powers from having been shot into the body of the owner while on war parties). This particular collar is unique in that it has attached at each end two pouches made of human scrota. In one was found hoddentin; in another, killikinik; the third contained chia seeds; and the fourth held a white vegetable powder which has not been identified. Somewhat similar necklaces are known to have existed among the Shoshone, Ojibwa and Sioux. (Fig. 2.)

Izze cloths or medicine cords were so sacred that the subject has been difficult to investigate for the Indians refuse to mention them. They were made of three or four strands of different colored cord. One end invariably contained hoddentin or chalchihuitl and the other end terminated in a circlet of reed covered by leather painted with symbolic figures and garnished with feathers. They were only worn on the most solemn occasions, being slung from the right shoulder, the pouch and circlet falling on the left hip. It was believed that bullets could not harm the wearer, that it helped crops and cured the sick. The circlet, if placed on the head, immediately stopped headache.

The tom-tom, familiar in the Indian lore of every American boy, was not used in the treatment of the sick; but the water drum had an important place in medical rites. The earlier drums had as their base large scooped-out logs, thick tanned hide vessels, or large pottery jars. The base was filled about two-thirds full of water and a drumhead of thin cured skin was stretched taut over the mouth. The drum sticks were like curved clubs or boomerangs; and with them the drumhead was rubbed, not struck. The resulting sound was a low-pitched, thunder-like rumbling. The waterdrums were used widely in the ceremonies which accompanied the treatment of the sick, and definitely heightened their soporific and hypnotic effect. (See Fig. 7.)

Harlow Brooks states that medicine pipes were used in rituals enacted over the sick in certain tribes. Mrs. M. C. Stevenson describes a Zuni ceremony in which pipes were utilized. Yet other authorities, notably Bourke, are dogmatic in denying such use of pipes. Such abstinence would be surprising in view of the important place the passing of the pipe held in most other social, religious and political activities. The large stone, pottery or wooden bowl and long stem, carved, tinted and decorated with feathers, is so familiar that it hardly warrants further description. The use of the pipe is a good example of the Indians' penchant for symbolism; for the stems of many ceremonial pipes were not perforated, and some are extant that have neither perforation nor bowl.

Besides these, there were many minor accessories of medicine practice and ritual which require only passing notice. Perhaps the most important of these were the rattles. One group was made up of anklets, bracelets and reed rings from

Fig. 2. Medicine necklace worn by the Cheyenne shaman High Wolf. There are eight left hand middle fingers of hostile warriors killed by the owner and five arrows which had been shot into the owner's body by the enemy. The two pouches containing medicine are made of human scrota. After illustration in J. G. Bourke's "Medicine Men of the Apache."

FIG. 3A.

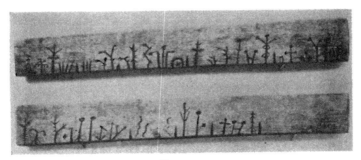

FIG. 3B.

FIG. 3. A. Wooden medicine bowl, Winnebago. B. Prescription stick, Potowotami. (Courtesy of Museum of American Indian. Heye Foundation.)

which were hung strips of hoof, horn or thick, tanned hide, which made stridulations by striking each other when they were in motion. Another type was made up of gourds, turtle carapaces, animal bladders or stiff leather sacks. The sound was made by pebbles or beans placed in the container. (See Figs. 7 and 8.)

Medical staffs called "calumets," medical arrows, wands, and spears were accessories in several tribes. They were highly decorated with symbolic colors, designs and feathers. (See Fig. 8.) The Chippewa used interesting medical poles which were set up before the lodges of the ailing to appease the spirit that sent the unpleasant visitation and to attract such spirits as might come to the aid of the invalid. They were saplings about 20 ft. long, stripped of their bark and brightly painted; bearing at the top tufts of feathers, died horse-hair or other ornaments. When there was an epidemic these ornate poles gave the village a falsely gay appearance.

Among the miscellany which should receive some mention is a unique piece in the Heye Foundation's collection. It is a Potawatomi prescription stick, a narrow ruler-like strip of wood on which are engraved representations of various herbs used by the owner (Fig. 3 B).

The famous "medicine bundles" of the Pawnee Picts and a few other plains tribes require a word of explanation as they are commonly assumed to be a homologue of the white physician's medical case. In fact, however, they were strictly part of the Indians' religious equipment. They were collections of sacred articles, kept at the family altar and passed down through generations of the same family.

# CHAPTER IV

## MORBIDITY

In considering the medical knowledge of the Indians it must be borne in mind that many of the diseases common under urban conditions were unknown to a race which lived in small groups, semi-nomadic, and surrounded by unusually good hygienic conditions. Civilized medicine has for generations been considerably preoccupied by contagious diseases and as a result of vast experience with bacterial disease has developed a technique of prevention and cure. What the white most scorned in the Indian's practice of medicine was his inability to cope with the recently introduced contagious diseases. The Indian had no racial immunity and when yellow fever, smallpox, measles or scarlet fever were introduced by a passing white the Indian community was decimated by the disease. Instances are recorded where a party of apparently healthy whites merely camped without so much as seeing an Indian, and the next year other travelers arrived and found the whole neighboring community wiped out and so rapidly that the woods and deserted village were littered with unburied bodies. In truth the Indian might more justly scorn a civilization that lived under such circumstances that plagues were sufficiently frequent to allow its physicians to become adept in treating infectious diseases.

Before the discovery of America the Indians may have had tuberculosis; but this is not certain. It has long been held that syphilis was of Indian origin and was introduced to Europe by the returning explorers. Recent discoveries and a more careful review of the archeological remains which led to this belief have cast grave doubts on the truth of the assumption. Certain it is that gonorrhea was unknown to the Indian before the advent of the white.

Neoplasms are not known to have occurred among the early Indians. The physicians who deal with the modern Indians state that, even allowing for difficulties of diagnosis, malignancy in pure Amerind strains is a great rarity.

Certain other diseases common to civilized communities were not understood by the Indians probably because of their lack of experience with them. These were obesity, arteriosclerosis, heart disease, endocrine disorders and insanity. Sporadic cases were recognized but were considered as curiosities.

On the other hand, in accord with their habitat and mode of life, other groups of diseases were common, and were usually well understood, at least, from the point of view of therapeutics. Digestive disturbances were frequent, due to two conditions. First, spells of semi-starvation alternated with periods of abundance, during which they grossly over-ate. Second, it was the custom on hunting and war parties, or when the village was moving through hostile country to abstain from food, not infrequently for several days at a time. These fasts were broken by an orgy of feasting. Rickets was fairly common, dependent on their dietary. The life of exposure led to a great amount of rheumatism and neuralgia, and in the Great Lakes region pleurisy and pneumonia were

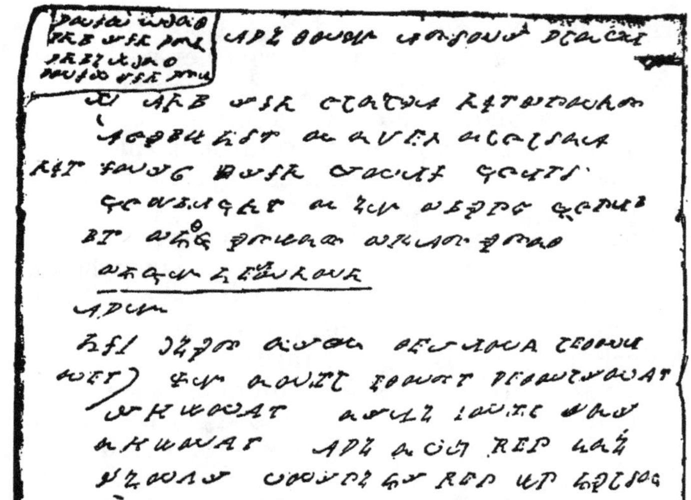

Fig. 4.

Fig. 4. Sacred formula of Cherokee. Prescription for treating a cripple. Written by Gahuni circa 1850.

TRANSLATION: "Yû O Red woman, you have caused it. You have put the intruder under him. Ha! now you have come from the Sun-land. You have brought the small red seats, with your feet resting upon them. Ha! now they have swiftly moved away from you. Relief is accomplished. Let it not be for one night alone. Let the relief come at once.

[Corner note at top.] If treating a man one must say 'Red Woman,' and if treating a woman one must say 'Red Man.'

[Prescription.] This is just all of the prayer. Repeat it four times while laying on the hands. After saying it over once with the hands on [the body of the patient], take off the hands and blow once; and at the fourth repetition blow four times. And this is the medicine Egû'ⁿlĕ [a variety of fern], Yâ'-na-Utsĕ' sta [Aspiduim acrostichoides or Christmas fern] two varieties of the soft [leaved] Egû'ⁿlĕ [one is the Cinnamon fern, Osmunda cinnamonia], and what is called Kâ'ga Asgûⁿtagĕ [Adian tum pedatum or Maidenhair fern] and what is called Da'yĕ-tuvâ'yĭ [unidentified]. Boil the roots of the six varieties together and apply the hands warm with the medicine upon them. Doctor in the evening. Doctor four consecutive nights. [The pay] is cloth and moccasin; or if one does not have them, just a little dressed deer skin and some cloth.

And this is the tabu for seven days. One must not touch a squirrel, a dog, a cat, a mountain trout, a woman. If one is treating a married man they [sic] must not touch his wife for four nights. And he must eat on a seat by himself for four nights, and must not sit on the other seat for four nights."

From 7th Ann. Rep. B.A.E.

frequent. The custom of living in lodges or tepees usually filled with smoke caused a great deal of trouble with the conjunctiva. In certain areas goiters and urinary calculi were endemic, as they are today in these regions among both their white and red inhabitants.

The Indians' very active life, their constant state of warfare, and the part played by the chase in their economy exposed them to an unusual extent to wounds, fractures and dislocations. In these fields of medicine they were remarkably efficient. In conjunction with this they had a knowledge of anatomy far superior to the average white contemporary.

# CHAPTER V
# SUPERNATURAL THERAPEUTICS

### DRUGS OF SUPERNATURAL PROPERTIES

The pharmacopeia of the Indian was made up of roots, leaves, herbs, barks and animal subtances. These fell into three classes: those having no action on the body, being efficacious purely because of their supernatural powers; those believed to be effective because they seemed to resemble the disease or the alterations which would appear on the surface to relieve the condition, the so-called "doctrine of signatures"; and lastly, those which were used for their specific drug action.

Chalchihuitl, hoddentin, kungue and killikinick were of the first group. The first of these is the ground powder of an impure malachite, known to the whites as turquoise. Among the Apache it was the medicine-man's diploma, none being allowed to treat the sick unless he possessed a bit of it. The ground powder was sprinkled over the patient during the healing rites.

Hoddentin was the pollen of thule, a variety of cattail reed, which grows in all the little ponds of the Southwest. It is believed to have been a prehistoric food; but has persisted in sublimated form as a ceremonial powder, its ingestion being in historic times only practiced as a rite. All plains Indians possessed it; part of their daily ritual consisted of tossing a pinch of it into the air while facing the sun on arising in the morning. It was widely used in the performances over the sick.

The theurgist, while repeating a prayer or bit of gibberish, sprinkled hoddentin in a specified manner over and around the invalid. If a brave was wounded while on a war party, a medicine-man walked before the wounded warrior's horse strewing the sacred powder on the ground to make the way easier. When fatigued a little hoddentin was taken by mouth as a restorative, although no actual effect of the powder, except a psychological one, is known to have taken place.

Kungue or powdered meal was ceremonially used by many of the tribes of the Southwest, especially the various Pueblo Indians in much the same way as hoddentin. Besides its use in ritualistic medicine, it was used extensively in religious observances. It was also used in the amenities of social life. Each dwelling had a dish of it by the main door, it being a matter of courtesy to sprinkle a bit of kungue on arriving and departing friends.

In comparative anthropology it is found that the use of such powder dates back to remotest antiquity, and is spread widely over the globe. At the present time, the Spaniards sprinkle a meal powder on each other at the church in their village festivities on Shrove Sunday. Many African tribes use a sacred powder called "uganya." Similar meals were used by the ancient as well as modern Peruvians. The modern devotees in India use a red powder in the same way; and the negroes of Haiti and New Orleans use ground meal in their voodoo mysteries. The American Indians of Virginia and the Navajo also used such powders.

Killikinick was the powdered leaves or bark of several plants and trees alone or in combination.

Willow, sumac, dogwood, bearberry, and silky cornel were all used in this way. It was used by the Algonkian as well as the plains Indians, being smoked with or without tobacco. As a medicine it was supposed to protect against malarial fevers.

### FETISHISTIC THERAPEUTICS

Where disease is supposed to be due to the entrance of evil spirits into the body it is common to find many articles and practices used as charms to prevent or cure disease. The Amerinds were true to type.

The Apache hung a small stick from the woody part of a spiny cactus called cholla (Opuntia emorcyi) around the neck of their children to protect them against sickness. If the community were threatened by an epidemic, a whole plant was placed before the lodge door and others placed around the hut at the cardinal points of the compass to ward off contagion. Many other tribes wore similar amulets to fend off illness.

While all ceremonial treatment of demonaic disease was directed toward drawing out or scaring away the offending spirits, the Tatu of Potter's Valley, California, devised an ingenious means of mechanically plucking out the "bad medicine." The patient, naked, was laid supine upon the ground with the limbs widely extended. Four springy twigs were then placed in the ground a short distance from his hands and feet, bent over and tautly tied to the extremities of the invalid. The shaman, spirally painted to resemble the devil, burnt the string, as he muttered appropriate incantations, with a live coal. As the string parted, the branches snapped upright, to the tune of the well coached patient's screams. In this way the evil spirit was twitched forth.

Another type of fetishistic practice was seen among the Mohave. When a child became afflicted with whooping-cough the father must perforce abstain from drinking tea, and had to bathe in the Colorado River at specified intervals. A vaguely similar custom was found among the Winnebago. Sickness was believed to be due to an unrealized desire and to exorcise this spirit of unfulfillment, the article desired had to be procured for the patient at all cost, whether it be a calico rag or a canoe.

Certain Southwestern tribes, as a last resort, made an altar of sand or clay near the moribund patient. Around the altar were placed effigies of the Beast Gods. These were incinerated to the accompaniment of appropriate chants and dances. The ashes were then sprinkled over the patient and on the attending physician.

Other fetishistic practices will be more fully described as they occur in the ceremonial therapeutics presented later. But one particular phase of occult practice should be mentioned here; that is treatment according to the "doctrine of signatures."

The Hopi seem to have been specialists in this branch of medicine as their therapeutics was rife with illustrations. Thus, they dusted hot ashes on inflamed, burning skin or touched such areas with live coals. Because of their hair-like fibers, clematis and cowania were used in treating for falling hair. In pharyngitis they gave decoctions of the many-spined thistle. Or a twisted piece of wood was laid by the theurgist on the body of a person in convulsions. They held in high repute bits of wood from trees which had been struck by lightning for use in fractures. The wood was not used as a splint, but was simply laid on the immobilized limb.

The use of parts of the bodies of rattlesnakes in the cure of snake bite was widespread. The Micmac and Penobscot of New Hampshire and Maine drank a soup made of the meat of the snake. Certain tribes of the Northwest covered the bite with the entrails of the reptile. Others applied pieces of the meat to the wound, some used the powdered rattle, several bound the fang marks, if on a limb, with the whole body of a rattlesnake, etc.

In some tribes, mothers with faulty lactation were given decoctions of milk weed. The skin of a weasel, an animal which glides easily through difficult channels, was always placed in the room where a Hopi woman was in labor. The Yokuts used infusions of the scrapings from bears' claws to facilitate difficult parturition. The Crees and several tribes of Oregon and Washington gave powders of snakes' rattles for the same purpose.

# CHAPTER VI

## LEGITIMATE THERAPEUTICS OF
## MEDICAL CONDITIONS

The Indians were keen observers and were adequate practitioners, so far as an empiric knowledge of disease would permit. When the nature of the ailment was understood, they treated the patient by drug and physiotherapy. In the majority of cases this was sufficient although the shamans had no knowledge of the specific action of their prescriptions and it is to be suspected that many of them had no such action. Drugs were usually administered in single large doses in the form of a decoction or an infusion. Powders and inhalations were, however, not uncommon. It was only when the disease failed to respond to these measures, or was obviously, to them, of a mysterious nature, or seemed to be mortal, that they had recourse to their more complicated rituals.

As a rule, when a medicine-man was called in, his medicines were administered to the accompaniment of prayer and chant. All Indians had some knowledge of the commoner remedies; but the more particular medicines known to the theurgists were carefully guarded secrets. In those tribes with scant theology and organization the medicine-men worked more or less individually and jealously kept their knowledge a mystery. The laymen were led to believe that the drugs came from far away; whereas, in reality they used local plants which they collected surreptitiously at night when the village slept. In other tribes even the common medicines known to all were only collected after appropriate offerings to the gods and prayers and chants. In those tribes which were highly organized certain medicines were under the proprietorship of the various medical societies, and the collection and preparation of the society's medicine were highly ritualistic. For example, the six herbs entering the very effective antirheumatic medicine of the Little Fire Fraternity of the Zuni required a four-day ceremony for their preparation.

A complete enumeration and discussion of all the drugs used by the several hundreds of tribes in the United States area would expand this book to unwieldly proportions. Therefore, under the headings of the various types of diseases, the form of the drug treatment will be suggested and a sufficient number of herbs will be presented to give a general outline of the medication.

### FEVERS

The Indians recognized the syndrome of a dry, hot skin, muscular pains, chills, thirst and prostration; but they did not know it to be a sign of bacterial invasion. They understood the prognostic significance of the moister cooler skin and of the cessation of thirst. Their management of the case included rest, sweating, purgation, diuresis and a diet restricted to liquids (in a few tribes a patient suffering any malady at all refused all food for the duration of the illness, a custom which in not a few cases resulted in death from starvation). The plains tribes and those bordering on the Great Lakes practiced phlebotomy in fevers, using a sharp piece of flint as a lancet. Many drugs were used, the specific actions of which were not understood,

but which had been found efficacious by the method
of trial and error. No doubt a number were of
benefit merely because the copious drafts forced the
fluids the patient was taking. A few of these drugs
appear in Table I.

### GASTROINTESTINAL DISTURBANCES

Gastric and intestinal disturbances were recognized only as pain, colic, gastric distress, flatulence,
nausea and vomiting and evacuatory disorders.
The etiology, except in the matter of dietary
indiscretion, simple colitis and ordinary constipa-
tion, was not understood. The reflex action of the
various digestive organs on each other and the
relation of renal to intestinal pathology and vice
versa was not dreamed of. As a result the therapy
was directed to the symptoms rather than the
disease, which is true of practically all Amerind
medicine.

For any form of gastric disorder they employed
emetics. In fact, the Indian took emetics as
frequently and casually as the white takes laxatives. In many tribes every one took an emetic
daily as a matter of common decency. In religious
observances, especially among the Pueblo Indians,
emetics were used by the priest as a symbolic
purification; much as the Christian priest washes
his hands in certain Catholic ceremonies.

All tribes knew the use of the feather in producing the desired result. Many ingested repeatedly
large quantities of warm water, emptying the
stomach several times during the process. The
medical lore of every tribe was rich in the emetic
roots and herbs, some of the more typical of which
appear in Table II.

TABLE I

FEBRIFUGES

| Common Name | Scientific Name | How Used | By What Tribes |
|---|---|---|---|
| Willow............ | Salix | Decoction of leaves and bark | Pima, Apache, Mohaves, Winnebago, Dakota |
| Watermelon........ | Cucubiter citrullus | Eaten raw | Penobscot, Micmac |
| Wild sage......... | | Decoction of the leaves | Cree |
| Quaking aspen..... | Populus t r e m u l-oides | Decoction of the leaves | Apache, Mohave, Winnebago, Dakota |
| Dog wood*........ | Cornus florida | Decoction of leaves and bark | Ottawa, Chippewa |
| Tulip tree......... | Liriodendron tulipifera | Decoction of the fruit and bark of the root | Delaware |
| Marsh fleabane..... | Pluchea fetida | Decoction of plant | Choctaw |
| Red grass......... | Andropogan furcatus | Decoction of plant | Omaha |

* The ordinary dose contained 30 grains of cinchona.

TABLE II

EMETICS

| Common Name | Scientific Name | How Used | By What Tribes |
|---|---|---|---|
| Holly.............. | Hex vomitoria | Long brewed decoction of scorched leaves | C a d d o, Comanche, Cherokees, Creeks, Seminole, Enchee |
| Cucumber.......... | Sicyos origonus | Decoction of the vine | Klikata |
| Thoroughwort........ | Eupatorium | Decoction of leaves | Choctaw, Creeks |
| Butterfly weed........ | Aslepias tuberosa | Decoction of plant | Winnebago, Dakota |
| Blood wort.......... | Sanguinaria canadensis | Decoction of plant | Iroquois |
| Spurge............. | Euphorbia | Chewed raw | Apache |
| Iris.............. | | Decoction of leaves | Penobscot, Micmac |

Fɪɢ. 5. Sucking disease from patient. Ojibwa.

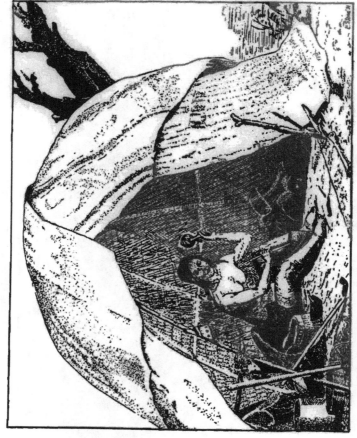

FIG. 6. Ceremonial preparation of medicine. Plains tribes.

The Indians of the Missouri River region (Dakota, Omaha-Poncha, Winnebago and Pawnee) used a few non-emetics in certain gastric disorders. Wild verbena (Verbena hastata) was taken for stomach ache. Infusions of wild mint (Mentha arvensis) were sweetened and used as a carminative. Prairie ground cherry (Physalis angulata) was employed for the same purpose, a decoction of the root being made. In cases of nausea they scarified the abdomen and applied powdered ragweed (Ambrosia elatior) which acted as a counterirritant.

Laxatives and purges were freely used by the Amerind. The salines were chiefly in the form of magnesia salts found in mineral springs and at salt licks. The laxative effect of bulky and cellulose stuffs in the diet was fully appreciated. The Tusayans used chopped bran in their bread; and most tribes, when the occasion demanded, ate leaves, fibrous fruits, husks of cereals and grass pulp. The Missouri River group of Indians and a few scattered tribes used enemata given by a syringe. This consisted of an animal bladder to which was fastened a nozzle of the hollow, cylindrical leg-bone of a chicken or turkey. Water was usually used, although the Dakota mixed with it pulverized bark from the root of the Kentucky coffee tree (Gymnocladus dioica). A partial list of Indian laxatives and purges appears in Table III.

In cases of colitis and various types of dysentery the Indians treated the most annoying symptoms, i. e., colic and diarrhea. For the relief of the latter they used the same medicines that were in vogue for that due to transient faults in diet. If the patient's condition became serious they resorted

TABLE III

LAXATIVES AND PURGES

| Common Name | Scientific Name | How Used | By What Tribe |
|---|---|---|---|
| American aloe......... | Cascara sagrada | | California tribes |
| Bush beans.......... | Agave americana | | Virginia |
| May apple.......... | Phascolus vulgaris | Beans were chewed | Penobscot and Micmac |
|  | Podophyllum pel-tatum | Ground root taken as a powder | Shawanese |
| Boneset........... | Euphatorium per-foliatum | As hot decoction | Ottawa, Chippewa |
| Sycamore........... | Platumus occiden-talis | Decoction of the bark | Winnebago, Dakota |
| Jalap........... | Convolvulus jalapa | Powdered root | Delaware |
| Slippery elm......... | Ulmus fulva | Fresh inner bark as hot decoction | Omaha-Poncha, Pawnee |

to theurgism. For the relief of abdominal pain, no matter what the cause, the Indians used massage, hot stones, moxas, hot poultices of ashes mixed with water, and the fleece of rabbits or birds' down as binders. The Omaha were more versatile, they mixed pulverized black rattle pod (Baptisia bractiata, Ell.) with buffalo fat as an ointment to be applied to the abdomen; or scarified the skin and rubbed in the powdered leaves| of Chamaesye serpyllifolia (Pers.). Other medicines for colic will be found in Table v, those for dysentery in Table iv.

### DISEASES OF THE RESPIRATORY TRACT

The common cold was differentiated by the Amerind from other respiratory tract diseases. However, the various types of bronchitis, lung infections and pleurisy were not recognized as separate diseases. So the Amerind used the same medicine in all conditions causing coughing or painful and difficult respiration. One exception was the Sac and Fox group which recognized pleurisy as such and were so far ahead of their time that as early as 1750 they treated pleurisy with effusion by incision and drainage. Consumption was unknown until introduced by the white. No specific therapy was developed, although the Choctaw, Creeks, Delaware and the New England tribes used a broth of rattlesnake meat in phthisis. The Pawnee and Omaha-Poncha gave decoctions of the whole plant of Sticky Head (Gundillia squarrosa, P.) to tuberculous patients.

The Indians of New England recognized asthma as a separate entity, and for the relief of this condition used Lobelia (Lobelia syphilitica).

TABLE IV
ANTIDYSENTERICS

| Common Name | Scientific Name | How Used | By What Tribes |
|---|---|---|---|
| Red medicine......... | Eriognum alatum | Decoction | Apache |
| Greasewood.......... | Covilla tridentata | Chewed and swallowed the gum | Pima |
| Seneca snake root.... | Polygala senega | Decoction | Nishinam |
| Oswego tea.......... | Monarda didyma | Decoction | Winnebago, Dakota |
| Cuchow-pint........ | Arum maculatum | Decoction of the bark | Iroquois |
| Low blackberry....... | Eubatus (foche) | Decoction of the root | Choctaw, Creeks |
| Red cedar........... | Juniperus virginiana | Drank the juice | Choctaw, Creeks |
| Geranium........... | Geranium maculata | Decoction of the whole plant | Ottawa, Chippewa |
| Red oak............ | Guvicus rubra | Decoction of scraped bark of the root | Dakota, Omaha, Pawnee |
| Wild raspberry....... | Rubus occidentalis | Decoction of scraped bark of the root | Dakota, Omaha, Pawnee |

A          B          C          D

FIG. 7. A, Waterdrum. B, Drumstick. C, Rattle. D, Medicine dish. All Menomini implements. (Courtesy of the Museum of the American Indian, Heye Foundation.)

TABLE V
INTESTINAL ANTISPASMODICS

| Common Name | Scientific Name | How Used | By What Tribes |
| --- | --- | --- | --- |
| Clematis | Clematis drumondii | Decoction | Apache |
| Greasewood | Covilla trodentata | Weak decoction of bark | Maricopa, Pima |
| French mulberry | Callicarpa americana | Decoction of root | Choctaw |
| St. Peter's wort | Ascyrum cruxandrea | Decoction of root | Choctaw |
| Mesquit | Prosopis juliflora | Decoction of powdered white inner bark | Papago |
| Indian corn | | Ground meal steeped in lye | Comanche, Kiowa, Blackfoot, Crows, Sioux, Cheyenne, Arapahoe |
| Beaver root | Heracleum lanatus (M) | Decoction of the root | Omaha-Poncha |
| Wild verbena | Verbena hastata | Decoction | Dakota, Omaha-Poncha |
| Sticky head | Gundilla squarrosa (P) | Decoction of whole plant | Pawnee, Dakota, Omaha-Poncha |

TABLE VI

DRUGS USED IN RESPIRATORY AFFECTIONS

| Common Name | Scientific Name | How Used | By What Tribes |
|---|---|---|---|
| Mesquite............. | Prosopis juliflora | Sap taken internally | Pima |
| Sassafras............. | Sassafras variofolium | Decoction of root | Nishinam, Winnebago, Dakota |
| Flax*............. | Linum usitatissium | Infusion of tops and leaves | Plains tribes |
| Skunk cabbage............. | Symplocarpus fetida | Decoction | Winnebago, Dakota |
| Red cedar............. | Juniperus virginiana | Decoction of nuts and leaves or burning of twigs as inhalation | Pawnee, Dakota, Omaha-Ponca |
| Holy plant*............. | Criodyctia glutenorum | Decoction as expectorant | California tribes |
| Bushy-weed............. | Ephedra viridis | Decoction of the tops, sweetened | Apache |
| Liverleaf............. | Hepatica triloba | Decoction | Delaware, Iroquois |
| Basil*............. | Pynanthemum albescens | Hot decoction | Choctaw |
| Sunflower............. | Heleanthus annuus | Decoction of the head | Dakota, Pawnee, Omaha-Ponca |

* In this and following tables those plants of proved efficiency are marked by an asterisk.

For the relief of pains in the chest, cupping was widely used over an extended area. The simplest form and the one having the largest vogue was scarification followed by suction by the mouth. Others, especially the plains Indians who had a copious supply of buffalo horns, used a horn with the pointed end knocked off. The skin over the painful area was scarified, the wider end of the horn pressed on the area and a vacuum was created at the small end by oral suction. Another type of cupping was done by placing a puff-ball or any one of the cottony parasites found on many trees, or a collection of spiders' webs in the open end of a horn, lighting it and clapping the open end of the horn onto the skin in the affected region.

Moxas were also used as counterirritants. The Pawnee took the comminuted stems of the lead plant (Amorphia canescens, Pers.), broke them short and applied them to the skin by moistening with the tongue; they were then fired and allowed to burn down to the skin. Any punk wood, animal dung, various plants with silky seeds, and spiders' webs were also used as moxas.

Table VI presents some of the drugs employed indiscriminately in all types of lung affections.

### CARDIAC STIMULI

The Indians knew very little about the circulatory system. Most tribes distinguished between arteries and veins and knew that the heart caused the flow of arterial blood. But very few drugs were consciously used for their cardiac action. We have been able to discover only four examples of the use of cardiac stimuli as such. The North Carolina

TABLE VII
DIURETICS

| Common Name | Scientific Name | How Used | By What Tribes |
|---|---|---|---|
| Sumac............. | Rhux copallina | Decoction | Most plains tribes |
| Wintergreen........ | Chimaphila maculata | Decoction | Winnebago, Dakota |
| Shrub yellow root.... | Xanthorrhiza apifolia | Decoction | Ottawa, Chippawa |
| Sarsaparilla......... | Aralia mediculilis | Decoction | Plains tribes |
| Juniper............ | Juniperous mona- sperma | Decoction of berries | Tewa |
| Magnolia........... | Magnolia macrophylla | Decoction | Plains tribes |

Indians used an infusion of holly (Hex vomitoria); Winnebago and Dakota exhibited horsemint (Monarda punctata); the Delaware administered Virginia poke (Phytolacea decandra); and the Pawnee employed bush morning glory (Ipomoea leptophylla, Torr.).

### DIURETICS

Dropsy was not uncommon among the Amerinds, and in their treatment of the ailment they realized the efficacy of diuresis. However, they did not distinguish between those cases of edema due to renal disease and those dependent on cardiac failure. They used various local applications on the edematous members; for example, the plains tribes applied tobacco leaves and the Winnebago used infusions of yarrow (Artemesia frigida). Scarification was practiced by many tribes. They discovered many diuretics to use in dropsy, a number of which are presented in Table VII. These were also used in any other disease where the urine was scant even if edema was not present; but the nature of such cases was not known and the drugs were employed because of their experience with them in dropsy.

### ANTIRHEUMATICS

Because of their dietary and their constant exposure to the inclemencies of the weather, the American Indians were unusually prone to arthritis, rheumatism and neuritis. They considered the conditions as phases of a single disorder and used the identical treatment for all. Because of their prevalence, the Indians developed a considerable armamentarium for their relief.

TABLE VIII
ANTIRHEUMATICS

| Common Name | Scientific Name | How Used | By What Tribes |
|---|---|---|---|
| Un-named cactus | Laphophora williamsii | Ground and powdered on surface | Tewa |
| Greasewood........ | Covilla tridentata | Tops used as a poultice | Apache, Maricopa |
| Balm of Gilead*.. | Pecca grandis | Applied locally | Miwok |
| Black birch........ | Betula lenta | Excrescence applied locally | Penobscot, Micmac |
| Jalap............. | Convolvulus jalapa | Slit root, heated, applied hot | Choctaw, Creek, Delaware |
| White walnut...... | Juglans cinerea | Bark as a local application | Choctaw, Creek |
| Bugbane.......... | Cimicifuga americana | Decoction | Winnebago, Dakota |
| Petroleum......... | | Wet dressing | Delaware |
| Sheeps' dung...... | | Hot poultice | Zuni |
| Fuzzy weed........ | Artemesis dracunculoides | Decoction of tops as a wash | Omaha-Poncha, Winnebago, Pawnee |
| Lead plant........ | Amorpha canescens (Pursh) | Moxa of bits of stems | Omaha-Poncha, Winnebago, Pawnee |

A  B  C   D        E

FIG. 8. A, Medicine arrow, Caddo. B, Medicine rattle, Kiowa. C, Medicine rattle, Comanche. D, Medicine fan, Comanche. E, Medicine dolls and wrappings, Menomini. (Courtesy of the Museum of the American Indian, Heye Foundation.)

Although used in almost all types of illness, sweat baths were particularly favored in combating neuralgias and rheumatism by all tribes. The Carolinian Indians buried the affected members in holes filled with hot mud; and also for several hours at a time had the children pour cold water constantly over the limbs. The usual moxas were freely used, as well as scarification and cupping. The Dakota and Omaha-Poncha had a very effective procedure: they applied the crushed leaf of pasque flowers (Pulsatilla patens) to the skin over involved joints, which was a sufficiently strong counterirritant to produce a large blister. The Pawnee burned the flowers of false lupine (Thermonsis rhombifolia, Nutt.) under such joints and covered fire and joint with a blanket. This fumigation rapidly reduced the swelling and eased the pain. Many kinds of washes and poultices were used. A list of internal and external remedies employed in these conditions will be found in Table VIII.

### NARCOTICS, ANODYNES, INTOXICANTS

The action of the indigenous narcotics and intoxicants were in general well understood, especially by the Indians of the Southwest. The red bean of Texas (Sophora secundiflora) was used to enhance the effect of mescal brandy. Or the red bean was taken by itself, half a bean producing a violent delirium followed by a sleep lasting two or three days. On awakening, there were no unpleasant after-effects. The Kiowas and the Fox and Sacs had organized societies built around the use of this drug.

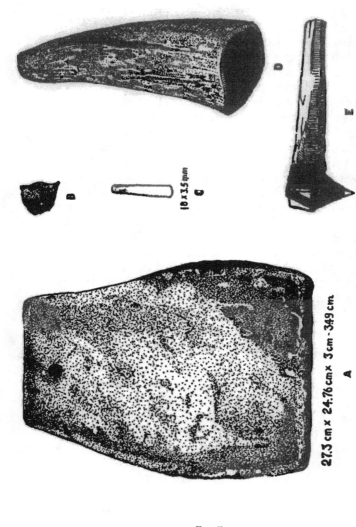

27.3 cm × 24.76 cm × 3 cm - 3.49 cm

**A**

Fig. 9. A, Steatite comal for applying heat, from Burton Mound, Santa Barbara, Cal. B, Flint used as a lancet. Chippewa. C, Gilsonite pencil for rubbing sore parts, from Burton Mound. D, Horn used for sucking after scarification. Chippewa. E, Lancet for phlebotomy. Chippewa. (After photographs in 44th Ann. Rep. B.A.E.)

The early travelers describe a mushroom used by the Indians of New Mexico, the decoction of the plant acting as an intoxicant. As no mushroom possesses such properties, it is believed that they referred to a mushroom-like cactus (Laphophora williamsii) which does act as an intoxicant.

"The devil's foot or peyote bean," miscalled the "mescal button," was used by the Apache, Comanche, and later, by the northern plains Indians in the same way as the Sophora secundiflora. One button produced a profound and pleasing lassitude with some dissociation of muscular activity, and in a short time brought beautiful hallucinations of swirling colors. The effect wore off in five or six hours with no unpleasant aftermath. The Omaha had a secret society devoted to the use of the peyote bean, like the Red Bean Society of the Kiowas.

The Daturas, a narcotic commonly called "Jimson" or Jamestown weed, was used ceremonially as a means of producing a holy delirium in the priests, in which state they were believed to be in communication with the spirits. In large doses it acts as an aphrodisiac; many of the tribes understood this property, the Mariposa giving it to the young women in certain ceremonial dances and to the youths in the ceremony initiating them into manhood. The Zuni used it as an anodyne. Mrs. Stevenson describes a rather extensive operation on a breast performed under its influence in 1891 during which the patient apparently suffered no pain at all.

Several tribes used infusions of certain plants to render the skin insensitive to heat, applied by the celebrants of their Fire Dances. The Zuni used yarrow (Achillea borealis) in this way. The members of the Heyoka Society of the Omaha chewed and rubbed the mucilaginous red false mallow (Malvastrum coccineum, Pers.) on their hands and arms before performing their feats of painlessly removing articles from boiling water with their apparently bare hands. The dancers in the Fire Dance of the Navajo ceremony, called the Mountain Chant, rubbed a white clay over their skin which, in conjunction with the low combustion point of the macerated cedar bark rubbed over themselves after ignition, prevented burns or blisters.

### TREATMENT OF CONTAGIONS

The aboriginal Indians had little or no experience with contagious disease. As they had no racial immunity, when introduced, these diseases spread like wild fire and were more effective in subjugating the savages than all the military expeditions sent against them. Europeans had only to camp in the vicinity of an Indian village; and time and again it was reported that on their return trip they found the village wiped out and with such rapidity that the lodges and woods were strewn with the bodies. And this despite the fact that none of the whites was ill or appeared to harbor any disease. During the Black Hawk war a soldier with smallpox was debarked from a troop ship near a Chippewa camp and within six weeks over two-thirds of the Chippewa in the entire region had succumbed to the disease. So terror-striken were the Indians by this type of disease that when smallpox appeared among the Paiutes of Owen's Valley, California, the members of the afflicted families were quietly put out of the way. Who murdered them or how, has never been discovered; they just disappeared. The sooner the family was eliminated, the sooner the contagion ended. In 1875 an epidemic broke out among the Dakota and it became the custom for those developing the premonitory symptoms to commit suicide by jumping into the Mississippi.

In time, however, they learned something of the nature of these diseases. Many tribes came to recognize that the incineration of everything with which the deceased had come in contact, hindered the spread of the disease. Among the Apache, Pima and Ute the hut and all the property of the patient were burned as soon as he died. The Navajo buried the body, with all his property, and burned the lodge. The Yuma and Mohave burned the hut, and consigned all the victim's effects to the funeral pyre. The Zuni buried the body, with his blankets, and threw away the extra clothes and bedding. The door of the abode was left open for four days, after which the floor was freshly plastered and the rooms white-washed before it could be reoccupied.

The Indians quickly distinguished the symptomatology of the various diseases; but in the main they treated the symptoms rather than the disease. Table ix presents the few medicines they considered specific in two of the contagious diseases.

### TREATMENT OF NEUROLOGICAL DISORDERS

The Indians knew little or nothing about the nervous system, and nothing about formal psychology. Yet they were remarkably successful in treating hysteria, as a glance at the case histories

TABLE IX

DRUGS USED IN SMALLPOX AND CHOLERA

| Common Name | Scientific Name | How Used | By What Tribes |
|---|---|---|---|
| *Smallpox* | | | |
| Petroleum.......... | | Wash applied to the whole body | Delaware |
| Sorrel.......... | Rumex verticillatus | Decoction | Choctaw |
| *Asiatic cholera* | | | |
| Cherry tree.......... | Padus serotina | Decoction of the bark | Ottawa, Chippewa |
| Red cedar*.......... | Junipirus virginiana | Decoction of the bark | Pawnee, Dakota, Omaha-Poncha |

presented later, will amply prove. This was due to
the happy accident that unwittingly made good
psychotherapeutics the basis of their all-important
ceremonial treatment of disease; and also to the
shrewdness and inherent understanding of human
nature that characterized their medicine-men.

In this section many conditions have been
arbitrarily placed which are not always dependent
upon neurological lesions per se, as headaches,
convulsions, etc. But in this the practice of the
Indians themselves is being followed.

Their moxa treatment of neuralgia and the
pungent fumes they used in syncope were effective.
Except for a rare alkaloid sedative among the
herbs used for headache, the balance of their
treatment of this group of disorders was chiefly
fetishtic, as the use of the izze cloth circlet in
headache; or according to the doctrine of signa-
ture, as the Hopi's use of a gnarled or twisted
stick laid on the body of a person in convulsions.
Table x presents a list of medicines used in these
conditions.

### SUDATORIES

The sudatory or sweat house was probably the
most universally used item of the Indian's medical
armamentarium. They repaired to it in each and
every malady and the more wealthy Indians
enjoyed it as a luxury.

All types of more or less hermetically sealable
lodges were used, tepees, earth mounds and skins,
grass or blankets covering bent saplings. The
principle was the same in any case: heated stones
placed in an enclosed space and drenched with
water to produce a dense steam. A few tribes

TABLE X

MEDICINE USED IN NEUROLOGICAL DISORDERS

| Common Name | Scientific Name | How Used | By What Tribes |
|---|---|---|---|
| *Headache* | | | |
| White man's berry............ | Lycium andersonii wrighti | Decoction of root internally | Apache |
| Pennyroyal.................. | Hedeorna reverchome | Aromatic twigs rubbed on hands and inhaled | Mescaleros |
| Red grass................... | Andropogan furcatus | Decoction applied to incision in scalp | Omaha-Poncha |
| White gilia................. | Gilia longifolia | Applied soapy wash of powdered leaves mixed with water | Tewa |
| Prairie ground cherry........ | Physalis lancolata | Decoction of root internally | Omaha-Poncha, Pawnee |
| *Neuralgia* | | | |
| Angel stem.................. | Heracleum lanta, mischx | Fumigation with root stock | Omaha-Poncha, Winnebago |
| *Syncope* | | | |
| Bush morning glory.......... | Ipomea leptophylla, torr | Decoction of storage root | Omaha-Poncha, Winnebago |
| Angel stem.................. | Heracleum lanta, mischx | Fumigation with tops and plants | |

merely dug a trench in ground that had been heated, the patient lying in the trench and covered by blankets, hot dirt or grass. (Figs. 10 and 11.)

Catlin gives a good description of the typical sweat bath as he saw it employed among the Mandans about 1832. All Mandan villages had a special tepee set up near a stream. Each family lodge had among its appointments a crib or basket of reeds, large enough to hold any member of the family in a sitting position. When any member of the family wished to take a sweat bath, the squaw carried the crib to the sudatory. Inside the sudatory were two stone walls 6 ft. long, 2½ ft. apart and 3 ft. high. Across the top of the walls rods were laid and the crib placed on these. Close by was an oven in a bank where stones were brought to a red heat. The patient or bather arrived, naked except for a blanket, and squatted in the crib. The squaw then brought in the stones, using a forked stick to handle them and placed them below the crib. She next doused the stones with cold water and then tightly closed the tepee. As soon as a profuse sweat occurred the bather emerged and plunged into the stream. This was followed by a brisk dry rub and a return to the family lodge where a long nap, under many robes, was taken.

### GONORRHEA AND SYPHILIS

The venereal diseases were another of the white man's gifts to the Indian, and were met with the same bewilderment that greeted the plagues. As regards syphilis, they did not recognize its systemic nature and believed the disease consisted of the primary sores and secondary rashes. These they treated with washes and powders (see Table xi). They developed no curative agents with the possible exception of Yerba mansa (Anemiopus californica). This is reputed to have been effective by white physicians who had occasion to see the cases in the third quarter of the 19th century, and probably was as efficient as the drugs then used by the whites. Unfortunately the antisyphilitic properties of the drug have never been investigated scientifically. It was used by the Maricopa and Pima.

Gonorrhea in the Indian had a tendency to remain localized in the urethral and vaginal mucous membranes, although occasional adnexal disease has been observed in both male and female. This apparently depended on a biological peculiarity rather than on any excellence of their treatment. They did hit on the importance of balsamics in the cure of the disease, but apparently used no douches urethrally or vaginally. They also used several active diuretics. Also, the Indian's method of taking fluid medicines favored this disease, as the quantity ingested effectively forced fluids. It was usual to take decoctions, a pint at a draught, although there was a tendency to consider one dose sufficient for the duration of the illness. Their antiblenorrhagics may be found in Table xii.

### TREATMENT OF SNAKE BITE

The Indians developed considerable skill in treating snake bite as it was one of the conditions which they frequently met. Although some of

TABLE XI
ANTILUETICS

| Common Name | Scientific Name | How Used | By What Tribes |
|---|---|---|---|
| Yerba mansa*......... | Anemiopeus californica | Decoction of root | Maricopa, Pima |
| Magnesia and sodium salts | | Mud or water containing these as paste | Plains tribes |
| Hazel nut.......... | Corylus americana | Inner bark powdered, dusted on sores | Plains tribes |
| Great lobelia........... | Lobelia syphilitica | Decoction | Choctaw, Creeks |
| Prickly ash........... | Xanthorium fraxineum | Bark chewed and applied to sores | Ottawa, Chippewa |
| Joint fir........ | Ephedra antisyphilitica | Decoction of leaves and stem | Pima |

* Known to be effective.

TABLE XII
ANTIBLENORRHAGICS

| Common Name | Scientific Name | How Used | By What Tribes |
|---|---|---|---|
| Thunder weed......... | Ephedra | The whole plant of both mixed and a decoction made | Mescaleros |
| Hard medicine......... | Holodiscus | | |
| Wild rose......... | Rosacea speciosa | Decoction of dried bud | Mescaleros |
| Oregon grape......... | Berberis aequifolium | Decoction of root | Klikata, etc. |
| Spruce......... | Picea canadensis | Vaginal fumigation by burnt twigs | Klikata, etc. |
| Seneca snake-root......... | Polygala senega | Decoction | Nishinam |
| Bearberry......... | Arctostaphylos uvaursi | Lotion applied locally | Plains tribes |
| Red root......... | Ceanothus ovatus | Lotion applied locally | Plains tribes |
| Sumac......... | Rhus glabra | Decoction of leaves internally | Plains tribes |
| Dogwood......... | Cornus alternifolia | Decoction of bark internally and locally | Plains tribes |
| Black haw......... | Viburnum prunifolia | Decoction of bark internally and locally | Plains tribes |
| Pine tree......... | Pinus (all varieties) | Decoction of bark internally | Winnebago, Dakota |

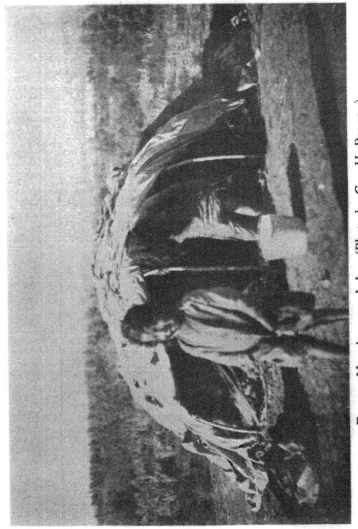

Fig. 10. Navajo sweat lodge. (Photo by Geo. H. Pepper.)

FIG. 11. Crow sweat lodge.

(Figs. 10 and 11 by courtesy of the Museum of the American Indian, Heye Foundation.)

their curative agents were fantastic, others had considerable practical value. They universally first applied suction at the site of the bite, many tribes excising the area. Some form of application was then made, varying from the purely fetishtic application of portions of a snake (muscle, rattle, or entrails) to the very effective Kuk-bi-ze of the Mescaleros. This root was plucked and chewed fresh, and the quid was applied to the bite and quickly reduced the swelling and pain, and in some way seemed to neutralize the venom. Other drugs used in snake bite are presented in Table XIII.

It is probable that the tribes of the Southwest which practiced the Snake Dance knew something, empirically if not theoretically, about immunization. In the ceremony the participants allowed themselves to be bitten by full-grown rattle-snakes, yet suffered no ill effects. As neophytes in the order, they had desensitized themselves by first submitting to the bite of young snakes with weak virus, gradually increasing the age of the snakes until they could receive the bite of the adult with impunity.

While much of their drug therapy, such as the drugs used in dermatitis, sore eyes, earache, toothache, their tonics, etc., have not been presented; certainly enough appears to give a good idea of their use of drugs. The list is apparently much the same as that which any old woman versed in the countryside herbs of almost any civilized or barbarous country might present if she were asked her lore. But when we turn to the treatment of wounds we enter on a field in which the Indian was an adept.

TABLE XIII

DRUGS USED IN SNAKE BITE

| Common Name | Scientific Name | How Used | By What Tribes |
| --- | --- | --- | --- |
| Peyote............. | | Sucked; poultice of chewed button | Tarahumare |
| Virginia snakeroot...... | Aristolochia supentina | Masticated and applied as poultice | Mascouten, Delaware, Iriquois |
| Senega snakeroot...... | Polygala senega | Chewed and applied as a poultice | Mascouten, Winnebago, Dakota, Delaware and Iriquois |
| Yellow dock.......... | Rumex crispus | Internally as decoction, externally chewed and used as poultice | Winnebago and Dakota |
| Common plantain...... | Alisma plantago | Chewed and applied as a poultice | Winnebago and Dakota |
| White ash............ | Fraxina americana | Decoction of buds, internally | Winnebago and Dakota |
| Aspen............... | Populus angulata | Steam from boiling bush and stem | Choctaw |
| Purple corn flowers.... | Ceniacea cenqustifolia | Chewed and applied to bite | Dakota, Omaha-Poncha, Winnebago, Pawnee |

# CHAPTER VII

## TREATMENT OF SURGICAL, GYNECOLOGICAL AND OBSTETRICAL CONDITIONS

The Indian women are, and always have been, so reticent about gynecological diseases that their medicine-men seem to know nothing about them and even the physicians on the Reservations can discover but little. Except for gonorrhea, it is believed that the Indian suffers relatively fewer disturbances of the generative organs than her white sister. One reason is that the full-blooded Indian baby is relatively much smaller than the white or half-breed baby. This is such common knowledge that in many tribes it is the custom to terminate pregnancies at the second or third month if a white is believed to be the father. As a result of the small size of the baby, the Indian mothers are spared the long train of post-partum disorders to which the white mother is prone.

However, the plains Indians, at least, must have occasionally been troubled by pelvic relaxations or malpositions of the uterus, as it is known that they used pessaries made of rolled buffalo hair.

Tumors, particularly cancers, were almost unheard of; but menstrual disorders, particularly dysmenorrhea, were probably not infrequent, as quite a number of remedies are known to have been used for their relief. These appear in Table xiv.

### OBSTETRICS

The nomadic tribes paid but scant attention to their pregnant women; but the village and Pueblo

71

TABLE XIV
DRUGS USED IN MENSTRUAL DISORDERS

| Common Name | Scientific Name | How Used | By What Tribes |
|---|---|---|---|
| *Leucorrbea* | | | |
| Geranium........ | Geranium maculata | Decoction | Ottawa, Chippewa |
| *Functional disorders* | | | |
| Seneca snake-root... | Polygala senega | Decoction | Ottawa, Chippewa |
| Black currant........ | Ribes americana | Decoction of root | Winnebago |
| Burning bush........ | Evonymous atro-purpurus, Jag. | Decoction of inner bark | Omaha-Poncha |
| Little wild sage...... | Artemesis frigida | Decoction | Pawnee, Omaha-Poncha, Winnebago, Dakota |
| *Dysmenorrbea* | | | |
| Smooth sumac...... | Rhus glabra | Decoction of fruit | Pawnee |
| | Gutierruzia longifolia | Squatted over smoke from coals of | Tewa |
| *Metrorrbagia* | | | |
| Smooth sumac...... | Artemesis frigida | Decoction of fruit | Pawnee |

Indians allowed them no over-exertion, prescribed frequent warm baths, and had the abdomen kneaded frequently to keep the fetus in a normal position.

Labor was relatively short, seldom lasting more than three hours, and was supposed to have been but slightly painful. In most tribes labor was conducted in a squatting posture. The Utes, Navajo, Apache and Nez-Perces assumed a semi-recumbent position. The Crow and the Assiniboine knelt, resting the head against a support, while a midwife pressed in the lumbar region during the pains. The Brule-Sioux and Warm Spring Indians stood throughout labor. Delivery was carried out with the woman kneeling, but she stood to deliver the placenta. In some other tribes this stage was conducted in bizarre fashion. The Coyotero Apache bound the woman to a tree as soon as labor began, with her hands tied to a branch above her head, and there she remained until labor was over. The Winnebago and Chippewa knelt over a bar, over which the woman was dragged, belly down, in case of difficult delivery. The Creeks lay prone with a pillow strapped to the epigastrium; as labor progressed the strap was tightened.

Most tribes conducted their labor in the family lodge, the members of the family departing when labor became imminent. The plains Indians built an inclosure of bushes apart from the village and near a stream. In this pen two stakes were placed and before each a hole was dug, soft earth filled one and hot stones the other. The woman squatted over the hot stones most of the time, and over the loose earth when discharges were passing, the stakes being seized during uterine contractions.

The Blackfeet, Unepapos, Comanche, Uintah and Cheyenne built separate temporary lodges for delivery. Among the Paiute, Brule-Sioux and Umpquas all the friends and relatives assembled to witness the performance; but in most tribes the woman was alone or assisted by one or two female friends or midwives.

The Nez-Perces alone of all the Indians used vaginal manipulations during the first stage; but only in prolonged labor. Fortunately this condition was rare, usually due to transverse position which not infrequently ended fatally. The midwives were adept in abdominal manipulations to correct the fetal position. If this failed, the maneuvers to facilitate the labor were almost as numerous as there were tribes. In most tribes the attendant knelt behind, locked her hands over the patient's abdomen and made downward pressure. The Dakota placed a wide strap around the abdomen (the "squaw belt") and tightened it. The parturient Sioux was taken, belly downward on the back of her helper, and was jounced about. The Cheyennes and Coyoteros-Apache suspended the woman by her arms, then clasped the abdomen from behind and squeezed and pulled down. The Nez-Perces turned the woman upside down and shook her; if this was not effective they inserted a hand in the vagina and pulled on whatever presented. The plains Tribes posted a man with a gun and at a signal he fired a shot, the fright sometimes expediting delivery.

All the Amerinds practiced Credé's method of expelling the placenta, at least a century before he published his procedure. The Kiowas, Comanche, Clatsops, Dakotas, Crow, Creek, Brule-Sioux,

Loafer, Agallala and Wazahzah also used the squaw belt. The Brule-Sioux, Warm Spring Indians, Crows, Creeks, Rees, Gros-Ventres, Mandans, Cheyennes, Arapahoe and Chippewa applied traction to the cord. The Crows, Creeks and Uintah used a post, with a blanket at the top against which the woman pressed the epigastrium. The plains tribes tickled the woman's nose, the sneezing causing the expulsion of the placenta. The Papago tied one end of a buckskin thong about the cord and the other end was bound to the foot of the woman, who made her own traction. A steam vaginal bath was used by the Misqually. In no tribe was the cord severed until after the delivery of the placenta.

The mortality both of mother and child was low. Dr. Feed, u. s. a., for six years in intimate contact with one tribe, knew of no maternal death and only one of a child. Another observer noted but one maternal death, due to transverse position, in 800 deliveries during a four-year residence with the Indians. Eclampsia, puerperal sepsis and post-partum hemorrhages were unknown. These statements are true only of the full-blooded Indians.

After parturition the Apache, Flatheads, Pend d'oreilles, Kootenous, Sioux, Santee and Skoko-mish observed no rest period. The Kiowa, Co-manche and Wichita rested a few days and wore a tight abdominal binder for some time. The Uintah woman lived in idleness in a separate "wick-e-up" for four weeks after labor. The Pueblo women remained on their pallets for four days, at the end of which time they were ceremonially purified at dawn by the priest.

The frequency of abortion varied widely, depending on social custom (where widows were not again married and had to support their children in event of the father's death) but more directly on association with white civilization. Where there was such contact, the delivery of half-breed babies was so difficult that abortion was practiced as a routine. So we find no abortion among most remote tribes, and unlimited abortion in the tribes that neighbored on the whites. Their methods varied widely. In a few tribes, friends stamped and trod on the woman's abdomen. In several others a board was placed across the abdomen and a woman sat on either end of it and jounced up and down. Slippery elm sticks were inserted in the cervical canal. For the drugs used, see Table xv.

Mammary disturbances were rare, abscess was unusual and was treated by fomentations or incision and drainage. The most common trouble was scanty lactation. The drugs used for this condition and as aids in labor are presented in Table xv.

### TREATMENT OF WOUNDS

Possibly because of the extreme frequency with which they were called on to treat wounds, the Amerinds became skillful in the art, just as the Italians of the 16th century became authorities on head wounds. Or it may be that the Indian possessed some sort of immunity to the usual infections that made wounds fatal to the white, just as the white had a racial immunity to pests that were fatal to the Indian. Or again, it is possible that the Indian possessed some mechanism

TABLE XV
DRUGS USED IN OBSTETRICS

| Common Name | Scientific Name | How Used | By What Tribes |
|---|---|---|---|
| *To speed labor* | | | |
| Rattlesnake (reptile).......... | | Powdered rattle | Klikata, Cree, Rees, Mandan |
| Bears' claws (animal).......... | | Decoction of scrapings from | Yokuts |
| Indian corn.......... | | Tea of blossoms or silk | Pueblo |
| Ground cedar.......... | | Decoction of the berries | Rees, Mandan |
| Pine.......... | Pinus mitis | Decoction of inner bark | Ottawa, Chippewa |
| Fir balsam.......... | Abies balsamea | Decoction of inner bark mixed with tobacco as a snuff | Ottawa, Chippewa |
| | Gutierrezia longifolia | | Tewa |
| *Dry breasts* | | | |
| Skeleton-weed.......... | Lygodesmia jiencea | Infusion | Pawnee |
| *Sore breasts* | | | |
| Milk weed.......... | Asclepias epeciosa | Infusion | Tewas |
| *Abortifacients* | | | |
| Rattlesnake (reptile).......... | | Powdered rattle | Klikata |
| Cedar sprouts, hops and bearberry.......... | | Decoction | Tulapis |
| Seneca snakeroot.......... | Polygala senega | Decoction | Ottawa, Chippewa |

by which the complicated biological action of
repair and protection acted more rapidly and
powerfully than in his white brother. Suffice it,
that all military and medical observers who came
in contact with the Indians agree that they recovered more rapidly than the white from most
wounds, and many recovered from wounds which
would have been fatal to the white man. Bourke
reports the cases of two Indians who were dis-
charged from a military hospital that they might
die among their people, yet made rapid recoveries
as soon as their own medicine-men began their
treatment. At a time when gunshot wounds of the
bladder were invariably fatal to the white, the
Indians seemed to suffer this accident with impunity. Loskiel examined a man whose face had
been torn away, his rib cage crushed, limbs ripped
and the abdomen disemboweled by a bear, yet
had been able to crawl four miles to his village and
in six months had completely recovered, except
for extensive scarring. Such records could be continued almost indefinitely as all observers were
so impressed by this ability to survive terrific
wounds that hundreds have been reported.

Although the Indians knew nothing of antisepsis, they understood the value of cleanliness
in the treatment of wounds. They had a further
advantage over their military opponents of the
first part of the 19th century and earlier, in that
they were treated individually in their own lodges
and so were not subject to "hospital gangrene"
which wreaked so much havoc in the military
hospitals of the day.

They dressed their wounds frequently and kept
them scrupulously clean (in this section the man-

agement described is that of the most skillful tribes). Many types of dressings were used, washes, powders, and poultices, all of which promoted free drainage; while salves, tending to seal the wound, were but rarely employed. From the herbs used it is readily seen that much of their success depended on their osmotic and absorptive powers (see Table xvi).

Many tribes, particularly the Tuscarora, Dakota and Winnebago used to suture the larger wounds with threads of sinew on bone needles, removing the sutures in from six to eight days. Inasmuch as their treatment was neither aseptic or antiseptic, they were unusually wise in their insistence that wounds should heal from the bottom by granulation. This they accomplished, when using sutures, by placing a thin membrane of bark between the cut surfaces before placing their sutures. Some Indians, particularly the Mescaleros, used twists of fiber or cloth as wicks for drainage. Most tribes contented themselves with removing only the more superficial foreign bodies; but the Tuscarora showed a skill in debridement and removal of even deep-seated arrowheads or shot that would have been creditable in 1918.

Their control of hemorrhage, granted a lack of knowledge of the ligature, was extremely rational as compared with many fantastic practices used by the Europeans at an era when they did not ligate. Most tribes knew the action of the cautery on bleeding vessels. The Mescaleros packed oozing wounds with eagle's down, or scrapings from the inside of fresh tanned hides (compare with the use of muscle tissue in modern brain surgery). The

TABLE XVI

DRUGS USED IN THE TREATMENT OF WOUNDS, FRACTURES AND DISLOCATIONS

| Common Name | Scientific Name | How Used | By What Tribes |
|---|---|---|---|
| Hellebore........ | Perezia wrightie | Cottony part of root to small wounds | Apache |
|  | Veratieim alba | Applied locally | Penobscot, Micmac |
| Silver pine........ | Pinus edulis | Oil of nut or pitch locally | Nishinam |
| Tobacco........ | Nicotina tabacum | Poultices of chewed leaves | Yokut, Micmac, Penobscot |
| Jimson weed........ | Datura meloids | Poultice of powder of blossoms or root | Yokut, Zuni |
| Alder tree........ | Alnus crispa | Application of chewed bark | Micmac, Penobscot |
| White pine........ | Pinus mitis | Turpentine from as wash, wood boiled or beaten to a pulp as a poultice | Penobscot, Micmac |
| Water lily........ | Nymphaeaceae | Roots applied to granulations | Penobscot, Micmac |
| Fir balsam........ | Abies balsamia | Pitch used as a salve | Celispels, Spokanes, Nez-Perces |

TABLE XVI (*Continued*)

| Common Name | Scientific Name | How Used | By What Tribes |
|---|---|---|---|
| Cold water............... | | Almost constant wash, especially in compound fractures | Dakota, Apache |
| Slippery elm............. | Ulvus fulva | Tent or poultice of bark, or mucilage from bark locally | Dakota, Choctaw, Creeks, Winnebago |
| Common elder........... | Sambucus canadensis | Bark as a poultice | Winnebago, Dakota |
| Hickory................. | Carya alba | Decoction of bark as wet dressing. Same used after second day | Delaware |
| Sarsaparilla............ | Aralia nudicaulis | | |
| Pennywort.............. | Obolaria virginica | Decoction of roots locally | |
| Sweet gum tree......... | Liquid ambar styraciflua | Gum rising on boiling roots mixed with above | Choctaw |
| Dandelion.............. | Taraxacum taraxacum | (In fractures) leaves ground fine, mixed with water as a paste, fresh leaves over this | Tewa |
| Wild rose.............. | Rosa pratinocola, G. | Growth on stems, scraped, charred and powdered on | Omaha-Poncha, Pawnee, Dakota |
| Pleurisy root........... | Asclyrias tuberosa | Chewed and applied or powdered and blown in wound | Omaha-Poncha |

Haidah packed the wound with spider's web and the Missouri River tribes either used puff balls for the purpose or made use of the styptic properties of smooth sumac (Rhus glabra). Almost all the tribes understood the use of the tourniquet.

### TREATMENT OF FRACTURES AND DISLOCATIONS

The Amerinds' care of fractures and dislocations was as excellent as that they gave to wounds. It was rare to find an Indian with a deformity following a fracture. Although they did not use counter traction, they were ingenious and skillful in arranging adequate immobilization.

Most tribes immediately set the broken bones and applied a splint of slats of wood. The slats were about 1½ in. wide, ¼ to ½ in. thick and long enough to immobilize neighboring joints. Near each end the slats were fastened to one another by thongs in such a way that they lay a couple of inches apart. The thongs were then tied around the limb, efficiently fixing it in position, yet allowing ample room for care of the contused or lacerated parts. Through the slats wounds were treated as though uncomplicated by fracture and contusions by decongesting and soothing washes or poultices (see Table XVI).

Some particularly clever splints were devised. The Shoshone made a splint of fresh rawhide. The leather was soaked in water until soft and pliable, then moulded onto the limb, after the fracture had been reduced. The surplus hide was trimmed away and the leather was bound in place by thongs. When dry the hide became an immovable cast as perfect as the best of modern plaster of Paris work. In the same way some of the New England tribes used strips of bark. Windows were cut in these casts to allow the treatment of compounded fracture. In comminuted cases the superficial fragments at least were removed.

They were also at home in handling dislocations. A few tribes did not understand hip dislocations, but in the vast majority these were as well treated as those of arms or digits. Indeed most Indians, even those who were not medicine-men, understood the required manipulations. Loskiel saw a hunter just after he had reduced a dislocation of his own hip. He was alone in the woods and had strapped the foot of the injured leg to a tree, and then by forcing himself away from the tree by his hands and his uninjured leg had succeeded in snapping the head of the femur back into place. They realized the importance of muscular relaxation, the Ottawa and Chippewa administering decoctions which nauseated the patient.

On the whole, their skill in the care of wounds, fractures and dislocations equalled and in some respects exceeded that of their white contemporary.

## SURGICAL METHODS

The Indians' surgery was of necessity limited, they knew nothing of asepsis or antisepsis, had only flint and stone instruments; and while the average Indian knew much more anatomy than the average white man of his day, the medicine-men did not possess a detailed knowledge sufficient to permit extensive surgery. The modern or recent Indian medicine-man who has had no formal medical training (there are about 600 Indians, graduates of reputable medical schools, who are practicing orthodox medicine today) is

not much further advanced than his archetype
of 300 years ago.

The aboriginal Indians amputated digits, but

A

B

C

FIG. 12. A, Instrument for pricking medicine into skin.
Chippewa. B, Spatula for powdered herbs. Chippewa.
C, Birch bark measure for liquid medicine. Chippewa.

not arms or legs. Boils were opened and phlebotomy was widely practiced. The Indians of the
Great Lakes Region incised and drained in empyema. In pre-Columbian days certain tribes had

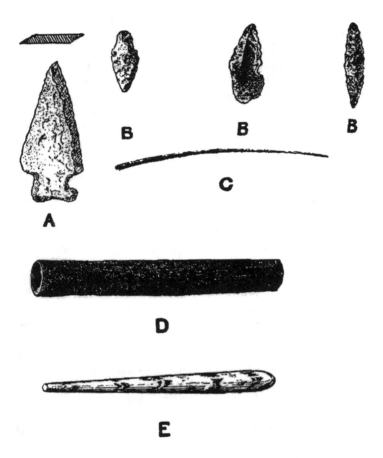

C. Stone, '31

FIG. 13. A and B, Flints used as scalpels and scarifiers, various tribes. C, Fishbone suture needle, Narragansetts. D, Bone suction and swallowing tube, Chippewa. E, Carbonate of lime tamponer, Apache.

practiced trephining, but by the 16th century this
had become a lost art. Beyond these simple pro-
cedures the Indians' surgery did not go. There is
one interesting exception. The North Carolina
tribes were the only ones on the continent that
understood the use of the ligature in controlling
hemorrhage; and the following account proves
that they also understood the use of the "skin
flap." To prevent their slaves from escaping, they
mutilated the unfortunate prisoner's feet. An
incision was made along the dorsum of the foot
at the junction of the toes with the foot and carried back to the head of the metatarsal bones.
Amputation was carried out at this point and the
skin flap rolled downward over the exposed joints
and sutured to the sole. Hemorrhage was stopped
by ligatures of sinew.

There follow two examples of more recent surgery by Zuni shamans. About 1902 Mrs. M. C.
Stevenson watched Naiuchi, a famous Zuni medicine-man open a breast abscess. Before operating
he gave the woman a decoction of Jimson weed
(Datura stramonium), which apparently put her
to sleep. The abscess was incised with a sharp
piece of flint and the cavity explored and its loculi
broken up by the operator's finger, a large quantity of pus being evacuated. During the performance the patient sat placidly, showing no signs of
discomfort and apparently asleep.

The same observer in 1896 became interested
in a girl nine years of age who had a curvature of
the spine and a cold abscess in the left groin. An
incision had been made for drainage, beginning
1½ in. above the posterior superior spine, trav-
ersing above the crest of the ileum and downward

almost to the internal ring. This was dressed frequently, the dressing consisting of removal of the previous packing, cleansing with water and repacking with pinon gum, kernels of squash seeds and mutton grease. A cotton bandage of many thicknesses was wrapped around the body. The patient died in a few months.

# CHAPTER VIII

## CEREMONIAL THERAPEUTICS

### RÔLE OF SLEIGHT OF HAND TRICKS IN THE SHAMANS' PRACTICE

One essential for the effective care of the sick is the patient's confidence in the powers of the physician. This spirit of confidence and awe the Indian medicine-men created by their application of theology to therapeutics, by the secrecy which surrounded their craft, and by the display of miracles which were in reality clever sleight of hand tricks. One of the chief functions of the Apache autumnal Medicine Dance was the impression made on the rest of the tribe by the marvelous tricks the celebrants performed during that part of the ceremony in which they paraded before the assembled tribe.

At a certain stage of the Medicine Ceremony of the Menomini an illusion was presented which never failed to excite the admiration of the candidates. The performer appeared, holding before him a piece of red flannel cloth, both sides of which were shown, to demonstrate that it concealed nothing. Then he bore it before him, held by its two upper corners. As he danced and sang, two snakes (or dolls or what-not) would gradually appear at the upper edge, would disappear and reappear again and again. What seemed to be a single piece of cloth was a bag. Between the upper corners a tape was stretched to the middle of which the figures were attached. As lateral tension was made at the corners the figures

88

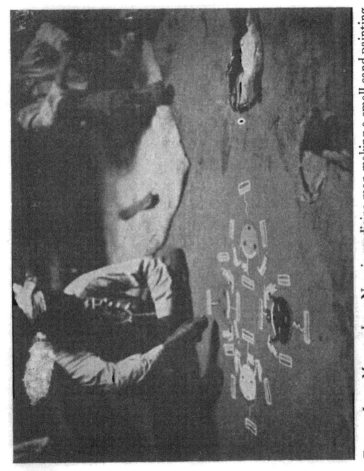

FIG. 14. Long Moustache, a Navajo medicine-man making a small sand painting (Photograph by Dane Coolidge. Courtesy of Mr. Coolidge and Houghton Mifflin Co.)

emerged through calico loops; and when relaxed, they fell back of their own weight. (See Fig. 8.)

The sucking of parts of the body to draw out the evil spirit was a widespread practice. To symbolize this, some object was removed from the shaman's mouth or, as among the Zuni, from the patient's body. So cleverly was this done that the Zuni theurgist could remove yards of cloth or yarn or bits of blanket; and even the white observer who recorded the ceremony could not detect the manipulations that made it possible.

The Walapi medicine-men had a peculiarly effective trick by which they seemed to demonstrate that they were people apart from other men. Where a group was assembled and the time and place seemed fitting, the medicine-man would announce that he had no further use for his intestines. Then and there before the eyes of the horrified audience he would draw from his mouth what appeared to be yards and yards of intestines. The mechanism was simple. Some hours before this form of hari-kari was to be practiced, the performer had rolled several yards of thread-like sinew into a small bolus. He had tied the free end to a small twig, fastened the twig between two teeth and had then swallowed the ball. After some hours submitted to the action of the gastric juices, the sinew had swollen to such proportions that it could readily be mistaken for intestines.

Another example of the Indians' magic is illustrated by the arrows swallowed in the key dance of the ninth night on the Navajo Mountain Chant, a medical ceremony. One-half of the arrow was made of a slender, hard twig of cliff rose; the other half of any pithy suffruticose herb. The

pith was removed so that the twig could move
into the cylinder like the parts of a telescope.
The herbaceous portion was so covered with
feathers that nothing could be seen of its surface,
nor of the junction between it and the wooden
shaft. An arrowhead was fastened to the free end
of the shaft, the arrowhead was placed in the
mouth and the cylinder pulled down over the
shaft, while to all appearances the shaft seemed to
be traveling down the performer's gullet. (Fig. 1.)

One peculiar feature of most of this chicanery
was that the artist seemed to believe in the spiritual nature as well as the efficacy of the deceptions just as much as did the hoodwinked spectator
or patient. Dr. Washington Matthews, who has
recorded the Mountain Chant in minute detail,
says that he has seen the jugglers practicing the
tricks, the arrow swallowing act being only one of
many. They were strong men and brave, but so
thoroughly did they believe in the supernatural
powers of their own deceptions that even during
the practice before the performance he has seen
the men trembling with fear and awe and looking
as pale as an Indian could look, from sheer
emotion.

### CEREMONIAL RITES OVER INDIVIDUAL PATIENTS

A study of the ritualistic medicine of the Indians
reveals that there was a subtle distinction as to
the source of the occult powers possessed by the
medicine-men in different tribes. In certain
tribes, as among the Zuni, the shaman was a
theurgist, that is, he was potent in expelling disease because the healing god had entered into his
body and he became for the time being a deity;

whereas, in most tribes, typified by the Apache, the medicine-man received his powers by special grant from some god, or through the possession of some sacred talisman or formula. He healed by the use of these deputed powers, not by identification with the godhead. However, this ideational distinction did not materially alter the medicine-men's technique; so the point will not be stressed in the following discussion.

The practice of the first group was conducted in a more rigid and unvaried formula by all medicine-men conducting a specific rite; but on the whole each medicine-man, especially among the non-theurgists, had his own personal ceremonial forms which were somewhat varied according to the needs of individual patients. In their essence all the rites were the same in that they were designed to exorcise the offending spirits, summon for their aid the benign spirits, and to put the patient in a receptive and hopeful frame of mind. These objects were achieved through prayers to those powers which might help, and the offering of acceptable sacrifices to them; and attempts to frighten away or draw from the patient's body the evil spirits. Specifically, these ceremonies entailed verbal insults to, rushes, leaps and kicks at the malignant spirits inside the sufferer, simulated attacks with spears or clubs on these spirits, and frightening noises, or suction to physically withdraw the demon. On the other hand these antics were interspersed with slow, stately rhythms of drum and dance, sonorous verses and prayers and pleading conversations in gibberish to inveigle the beneficent spirits to exert their power.

The medicine-men seldom worked alone, but with one or more assistants, sometimes the major part of the tribe joining the shindig and usually most of the patients' relatives and friends appeared to assist at the rites. An assistant would keep up a constant rumble of water drum or play of rattles, the depth and tempo of which he changed to match the actions of his chief. The chief would begin the ceremony by chanting a prayer to which the assistant replied in antiphonal phrases. Then all who had gathered would join in long choruses which rose and fell in monotonous cadences. Other songs and prayers would be interspersed by monologues in mumbojumbo, in which the medicine-man was supposed to converse with the gods. During all this the leader was dancing, and using his sacred spear, or rhombus or rattle or displaying his special sacred fetishes. The sacred powders would be sprinkled over the patient, or the sacred medicine administered or actual medicines given. These rites were continued until there was a change in the patient's condition. Occasionally the patient rewarded the combined efforts of friends, relatives and medicine-men by promptly dying. But, as the whole performance, in the main, was conducted in rhythmic, monotonous and soothing tones and movements, he usually fell into a quiet, hypnotic sleep from which he awoke hours later, much refreshed and benefited, sure that he was on the road to recovery and much impressed by the ability of his medical attendant.

There are dozens of variations on this general theme. In a Shoshone medical pow-wow there were from 6 to 50 or more persons gathered in the lodge, all provided with short clubs with which they beat on cubes or pieces of board placed in the ground before them. As the pounding was going on, they made a doleful howling and lamentation. This might be carried on for hours, while the medicine-man made ominous strokes and passes over the patient, took sacred water in his mouth and blew it in a fine spray over the patient. At last he announced that he had removed the source of the disease and that the patient would recover.

The medicine-man of the Gros-Ventres stripped the patient and went over the prostrate form, going through a series of gyrations and contortions, touching the patient with his hands, blowing on him, and chewing herbs and expectorating them over the invalid. While the shaman was at work, a limited number of assistants were beating drums and shaking rattles. After a long time the medicine-man would announce that he had heard the evil spirit, who admitted defeat and promised to depart. Or he might surreptitiously place a bit of charred wood in his mouth, suck the site of the pain and then display the cinder as the remnant of the spirit thus drawn out.

In many tribes much more formal and ritualistic ceremonies were carried out, such as those of the Navajo or Zuni. The Mountain Chant of the Navajo took nine days to complete. A special lodge was built for the ceremonies of the first nine days and eight nights, that of the ninth night was conducted in a corral some 60 yards in diameter and built in a circle about a central, huge bonfire. The walls were of boughs and stood about 8 ft. high. A small space was left as an entrance at the easternmost limit of the ring. The ceremonies for each day were carefully prescribed and had to be carried out with scrupulous care for each traditional detail. It involved the construction on various days of dry or sand paintings representing phases of the legend from which the ceremony evolved and picturing the various gods who were to aid in the curing of the disease. (Fig. 14.) Except for the last night, scarcely a word, gesture or position but had its symbolic meaning. The final night centered around the Dance of the Great Plumed Arrows which was the high point of the nine days' therapeutic ritual. There were, on this evening, many other dances added as the maker of the program saw fit or the neighboring talent permitted, but they were non-essentials. They were more or less for the entertainment of the crowd which had gathered to witness or assist in the final night. They varied greatly, ranging from burlesque acts to the drama of the Fire Dance, from the wild and graceful dances of gifted individuals to the superb beauty of the Dance of the Standing Arcs or involving acts which were clever illusions such as the Sun Show or that of the Yucca plant. The last act ended at dawn.

The Dance of the Great Plumed Arrows usually occurred early in the evening. In this there were two performers. They were naked except for a breech cloth of red flannel held on by a girdle of silver bosses. Their lower legs and their forearms and hands were painted black on which stood out the conventional "lightning" design in white. The rest of their bodies, including their faces, were daubed with white. A single eagle feather hung from the crown and the hair was worn loose. As the performers entered the sacred circle the patient

Fig. 15. Blackfoot medicine-man in yellow bearskin hung with parts of animals also showing anomalies. (After Catlin.)

was placed on a buffalo robe to the west of the fire
and directly in front of the musicians. Around the
edge of the circle were grouped the spectators,
sometimes hundreds in number. The performers,
having carried out the ceremonial circuit of the
fire, stopped before the patient. Each seized his
great plumed arrow between thumb and forefinger
of the right hand at the junction of the two sliding
posts, and with a yelp held the arrows up to the
inspection of the audience and the gods, then each
appeared to thrust the arrow slowly and painfully
down his throat. While the arrows appeared to be
stuck in their gullets, they danced a slow, shuffling
chassé. With difficulty the arrows were withdrawn
and triumphantly flourished aloft as the dancers
yelped in exultation. The sympathizing audience
yelled in response. Then one of the dancers
approached the patient to the soles of whose feet
he pressed the arrowhead, directed first to the
right, then to the left; so that two applications
were made to each foot. In the same manner he
touched the knees, abdomen, chest, back, shoulders, crown and mouth, in order named; and with
each touch yelped like a coyote. The second
performer then went through the same procedure.
When both had completed this ritual the patient,
still on the buffalo robe, was removed while the
two arrowbearers again danced around the fire and
left the sacred circle. This ritual cost the patient a
pretty penny as the patient had to pay the
medicine-man who conducted the affair, his
assistants, the musicians and the performers in
the different dances and acts. The one witnessed
by Dr. Matthews, from whose description this is
taken, cost the patient $250.00. (See frontispiece.)

The variations on these ceremonies by the several tribes and the individual medicine-men could be presented in almost countless numbers. But a few actual examples may be sufficient to make clear the nature of this phase of the Amerinds' practice of the healing art.

The first is that of a patient who was treated by a famous Blackfoot medicine-man called Petewaruxti (Wonderful One) during the first quarter of the 19th century. The patient was a woman who had been sick for some time and finally startled her family by remaining unconscious for twenty-four hours. It was then that Petewaruxti was called in. While his assistant rolled the water drum, the shaman sat silent by the patient for a long time. At last he moved, put his mouth to her head and began to suck. He sucked for a long time, until he seemed suddenly thrust away from the patient. When he finally regained his balance he spit a stone out of his mouth. Then he and his assistant carried her down to a brook which ran through the village. There they held the woman under the water until she began to struggle. When they released her, she walked home, a well woman.

Petewaruxti was called to see another woman, and as soon as he saw her he said she was not sick, but had the spirit of a horse. He mixed mud with stallion's urine and covered her body with it and put a streak of the paste over her forehead and nostrils. Then he took from his medicine bag a quirt made of downy feathers. With this he whipped her until she suddenly began to neigh like a horse. In a few days she was entirely well.

In 1830 a Blackfoot brave had been shot twice in the stomach at close range by a Knistineaux warrior, and seemed to be on the point of death. So heroic measures had to be used. George Catlin reports the incident, which he witnessed. The spectators, several hundred in number, gathered around the dying man, leaving him in a space some 40 ft. in diameter, and at one side leaving a path so that the medicine-man could enter the circle without touching anyone. In a few minutes the medicine-man's approach was heralded by a hush throughout the crowd. There was dead silence as he cautiously and slowly crept into the circle in crouching pose and lilting steps. His head and body were entirely covered by a yellow bear skin, the head of which served as a mask, and the paws dangled from his wrists and legs. This color of bear skin was an anomaly; and to the fur of it were attached dozens of skins or parts of animals that showed unusual deformities, snakes, birds, bats; beaks, toes and tails of birds; hoofs of deer, goat and antelope; and other similar objects. In one hand the medicine-man carried a gourd rattle and in the other brandished his medicine spear. As he approached the recumbent figure he suddenly burst into wild activity, shaking his rattle and emitting the appalling grunts, snarls and growls of a grizzly. These he intermingled with loud cries, ejaculations, and gutteral incantations to the gods. The din was made terrific by the screams, shouts and yelps of the entire audience. All the while the medicine-man danced around, rushed at and leaped over, pawed and rolled the patient. With his spear he thrust at the evil spirits in the sick man, or waved the spear over the body. The riot lasted about half an hour, ending only with the death of the patient. (See Fig. 15.)

The patient was a young man of the Zuni Pueblo in New Mexico who was suffering from a severe attack of sore throat. The following theurgistic treatment was witnessed by Mrs. M. C. Stevenson in 1891.

The Zuni are organized in several societies dealing in mystery medicine, in which a cure is effected through the agency of the gods of the society who enter into the bodies of the ministrants. Through this divine interference the evil spirit causing the disease is withdrawn from the body in various ways depending on the myth of origin of the different societies, in one by sucking, in another by removal by the hand, in the one here described by absorption into a cake, which is then eaten by a dog. The following rite was that of the Great God Division of the Great Fire Fraternity. It is always performed in the same way; and the success of the Fraternity in curing sore throats had almost made them specialists in that field. The components of the liquid medicine used was a closely guarded secret and the observer was unable to learn its nature. The origin of the ceremony is found in a myth involving the Great God, "Kok'kohlanna," his aid, "Shitsukia," and a lesser god, "Kewelele." They appear as the major characters in the ritual.

About sunset the members of the order assembled in the room of the patient, who was laid, reclining in the arms of his "fraternity father," on a rug in the center of the floor. Three theurgists wearing the costumes and masks of the three gods entered the room from the roof, led by a female member bearing a mili (insignia of membership in the order) and a basket of sacred meal. They

FIG. 16. Sore throat ceremony of the Zuni Great God
division of the Great Fire Fraternity.

Patient supported by his Fraternity Father on mat. The
theurgist representing the god "Kok'kohlanna" stands
before him. "Shitsukia" sprinkles sacred pollen on the
patient, standing at the patient's left. The representative
of "Kewelele" stands at the patient's right. To the rear at
patient's right is the female member bearing the basket
of sacred pollen. At the back, seated against the wall is the
chorus and the drummer. Other members of the order are
seated against the other walls. The altar insignia appear in
the central upper panel. In the other upper panels are
mili or feather decked ears of corn, insignia of membership
in the order. In the side panels are prayer plumes. The
central lower panel shows a Zuni medicine bowl and the
bottom side panels show fetishes of the several sacred
animals. (After painting by the author.)

Fig. 16.

[103]

circled the patient from left to right three times;
then Shitsukia, standing at the patient's left side
sprinkled the sacred pollen in a line from the
patient's left shoulder to the right groin (see
Fig. 16). Kok'kohlanna, who stood at the foot of
the patient, then waved a bundle of yucca over
this line. The gods again danced around the
patient and another line was made, this time from
the right shoulder to the left groin; and the yucca
leaves waved over it. The circling and drawing of
lines on the body were repeated according to a
rigid formula, various parts of the body being so
treated until seven applications had been made.
Kok'kohlanna then removed his mask, handed it
to the fraternity father who placed it over the
invalid's head. After the patient expectorated
through the small opening representing the
mouth; it was returned to the theurgist who again
donned the mask. During the entire ceremony a
choir kept up a continual chanting, to the accompaniment of rattle and water drum.

At this point, all the members of the fraternity
except the gods, the woman who led them in and
the fraternity father, left for their evening meal.
Those remaining were served by the patient's
relatives.

The members returned about nine o'clock and
consumed the remainder of the night in various
group and individual dances. In the dances the
gods were impersonated by numerous different sets
of members as designated by the fraternity
director. The women wore the costumes of the
gods but were not allowed to wear the masks. At
dawn the patient was placed near the north wall
of the room, and to the west of the choir. In the

center of the room Kewelele lighted a fire with his
fire sticks and cedar brand. An ember from the
fire was doused in a bowl containing the medicine
sacred to the fraternity. Kok'kohlanna carried the
bowl to the patient who took several draughts of
the liquid (the rest he used after the ceremony
was over).

Kok'kohlanna and his aid then took their
departure, but Kewelele remained. He held in his
right hand the fire drill and in his left the fire stick
and four cakes (three like doughnuts and the
fourth a perforated disc) strung on a yucca ribbon.
With these articles in his hands he made numerous
passes over the patient's body in prescribed order
and directions, and finally laid the string of cakes
on the patient's heart. The god then joined his
fellows on the roof, and with their attendants the
group left the village, going to a sheltered place to
the east of the Pueblo. Theoretically the gods were
departing to their home in the distant east from
which they had come at the call of the fraternity.
In reality the gods removed their costumes in the
copse and the attendents carried them concealed
under blankets to the room of the fraternity.

After the gods had left, the fraternity father
gave the cakes to the invalid who ate the ring
shaped cakes and tossed the one in disc form to a
stray dog who had been brought in for the purpose
by the mother-in-law (or some close female
relative on the maternal side). The wife of the
fraternity father (or closest contemporary female
relative) placed a bowl of yucca suds near the
patient. As the fraternity members filed out, each
scooped up a handful of the suds and poured it on
the patient's head, after which the head was

washed by the fraternity father. If the patient was not already a member of the society this ceremony made him one, without further initiation.

As payment the family of the patient gave a feast to the members of the order and rewarded the fraternity father with gifts of shirts, blankets, etc.

### CEREMONIAL RITES IN GROUP THERAPEUTICS

Many tribes conducted ceremonies in times of plague with the object of protecting or curing the entire tribe. And in another large group of tribes in which medical societies had developed there was a wholesale treatment of the ailing at certain meetings, especially initiation ceremonies of the societies.

One example of the former is found in a short description by a missionary named Mermet who, in 1700, was working among the Mascoutens near Fort Vincennes on the Wabash. During his stay some form of epidemic broke out among the Indians, which carried off large numbers of them. Their medicine-men, in an endeavor to check the epidemic, "removed to a short distance from the fort, to make a great sacrifice to their manitou. They killed nearly 40 dogs, which they carried on the top of poles, singing, dancing and making a thousand extravagant gestures."

In 1887 a band of Chiricahua Apache were confined as prisoners at Fort Marion (St. Augustine, Fla.). An epidemic broke out invaliding about half the band and causing the death of 23 children. At last the medicine-men decided to hold a "cha-ja-la." The preliminaries were almost as

important as the ceremony itself and both were
directed by Ramon, the oldest medicine-man, who
drummed and chanted from the first application
of paint till the last ministrations were completed.
The ritual began with the adornment of the three
shamans who were to be the actors in the dance.
They all wore undercoats of greenish brown. On
their bare upper arms were painted a yellow snake,
head over the deltoid; and a red flannel ribbon
was bound on below this. On the breast and back
of each jacket were painted various insignia about
4 in. in diameter. On the breast of one was a
yellow bear, and on his back a khan; bear and
zigzag lightning adorned the second, while the
third was decorated, front and back, with the
conventional lightning design. Each wore a
different mask and each bore a wand in either
hand, about the proportions of a common lathe,
with a snake lightning design on both flat surfaces.
When ready, the medicine-men began a peculiar
whistling as they bent slowly left and right; then
backward and forward until the head was at a
level with the waist. In this position they spun
rapidly in a circle on the left foot and then in the
reverse direction on the right foot. Immediately
they scattered and charged around, in and about
the group of tents occupied by the band, making
cuts and thrusts with their wands, to drive out the
evil spirits. Then they joined and visited a squaw
who held a papoose on a cradle. The mother
remained kneeling as they frantically beat about
the baby with their wands. Then the squaw held
the cradle up to the four cardinal points and at
each point the play with the wands was repeated.
At each point, after the passing of the wands the

baby was given to each medicine-man who held it to his breast, lifted it to the sky, lowered it toward the earth and then held it out to each of the cardinal points. All the time and during all this maneuver the medicine-men were whistling, snorting and prancing to the rhythm of Ramon's drum. The mother and friends of the patient's family added to the noise by shrieks and cries. Each invalid was visited and the same procedure was carried out over each.

The initiation ceremony of the O'Naya'nakia (those who heal by sucking) Order of the Ma' Ke Hlan nak we (Great Fire) Fraternity of the Zuni is an example of the second type of group therapeutics. The account presented here is extracted from Mrs. M. C. Stevenson's description of the ceremony as she witnessed it in November, 1891 Its performance consumed two days and fou successive nights.

The first day was occupied in setting up and decorating the altar in the fraternity room, the laying of the sand painting before the altar and in the construction of prayer plumes and the mi'wachi (the insignia of membership) to be given to the initiates. By nine o'clock in the evening the preparations had been completed and the members of the society, guests and patients seeking help had all assembled in the room. The members were busy adorning themselves. Both sexes had the arms and lower legs bare, which they painted white. The women wore their ordinary costume, minus the pin'ton. The men were naked except for black wool breechcloths. The women to be treated were grouped along one side of the room with their lower legs, the arms and neck bare, while the male patients were gathered along the opposite wall, wearing only breechcloths.

Sacred meal in corn husks was passed to each member who sprinkled it on the altar while he sang a propitiatory chant to the accompaniment of drum, rattle and flute. A large bowl of sacred water was consecrated amid the deafening roar of the rhombus. Ashes were then removed from the sacrificial fire and scattered over the audience by two performers who dipped the ashes with eagle feathers and with a fluttering motion distributed them in clouds. They then threw some to the cardinal points, the zenith and the nadir. Their steps and their manipulation of the eagle plumes and ashes were in accordance with a set formula which converted this ritualistic purification of those present into a peculiarly beautiful dance. The last phase of the dance was a similar sprinkling of water dipped with their feather fans from the sacred bowl.

The next feature of the program was the healing of the sick. An old woman took her place just south of the fire and at her side a large empty bowl was placed. The numerous healers stepped from the crowd of fraternity members and began to dance before the altar in order to impregnate themselves with the spirits of the gods. As the tempo and volume of the choir became greater and greater the dancers' pace and extravagance of gesture became wilder and wilder until the whole group was a mass seething in a religious frenzy. As the theurgist felt himself overcome by the spirit of the gods within him he would dash from the mass and with remarkably graceful movements stoop or throw himself almost prostrate to suck

at some exposed part of a patient. After a few
moments he would spring upright, eject something
into his hand, wave it aloft with shouts of triumph
and rush to deposit it on the bowl presided over
by the beldame. She presented him with a bowl of
the sacred water, from which he took a mouthful,
gargled and expectorated it into the large bowl,
then dashed away to treat another case. As more
and more left the group of dancers and flung
themselves among the patients the scene became
an indescribable kaleidoscope from which rose a
bedlam of cries, yelps, shrieks and always the
furious beat of the drums. Sometimes two or three
theurgists would be sucking at one patient. The
men were on the whole more graceful, but no less
violent than the women healers. This continued
for an hour until all the patients had been treated,
many several times.

This part of the ceremony was followed by the
first phase of the initiation of the novices, a fixed
and colorful ceremony lasting several hours. At
the end of this the purification with ashes and
water was repeated. Then all but the very ill stood
and intoned a prayer. The prayer closed about two
in the morning when the male members gathered
at the altar to sprinkle it with the holy meal and
receive a draught of the sacred water. When they
were done the women members gathered and did
likewise. Then the women left, to sleep in their
homes; but the men remained and slept in the fraternity rooms. The contents of the bowl which had
received the evil spirits drawn from the patients
were removed and buried with fitting observances.

The performances of the second night were more
organized than those of the first, but were initiated

by identical ceremonies of consecration of the water and sacrifices to the altar and purification of those present. The patients were garbed as before and the members wore the same costumes; but the women had red downy eagle feathers attached to the forelock, while the bodies of the men were painted in white zigzag lines to represent lightning.

At 10 o'clock a warrior dances before the altar, not moving from the spot on which he first stands. He holds an eagle wing plume in each hand, which he extends alternately toward the altar. After a time he dips the plumes in the medicine-water and sprinkles the altar, afterwards sprinkling to the six regions. Two theurgists now leave the choir and dance wildly before the altar, afterward dashing madly about, growling like the beasts they represent. (On this evening the Beast Gods are invoked.) They are soon joined by two female theurgists. The warrior then whirls the cloud cluster surmounted by A'chiy ala'topa (a being with wings and tail of knives), which is suspended above the altar, by touching it with his eagle plumes held in his right hand, that the clouds of the world may gather over Zuni. He also sprinkles the altar and choir, and sprinkles the women twice by dipping his plumes into the medicine-water. After the theurgists, who are now on the floor, have formed in two files, three in each, and have faced first north and then south, the warrior gradually becomes wilder in his gesticulations before the altar, bending until he almost kneels before it, which he leaves every now and then to join the dancers or to heal the sick. A guest from the Pueblo of Sia, who belongs to the Fire Fraternity of the pueblo, goes to the fireplace and stamps in the fire and literally bathes himself in the live coals. He then takes a large coal in his right hand, and, after rubbing his breast and throat with it, places it in his mouth. Others of the Fire Fraternity also play with the coals, rubbing them over one another's backs. As the night wanes the cries of the theurgists become louder and louder, and the time of the dance becomes faster. The women are as wild as the men. Mothers move their infants' tiny fists in time with the rattle, drum and song. The men keep their upper arms rather close to their sides as they raise their hands up and down. The lines of dancers often break into a promiscuous mass. Now and then a man drags a woman to the floor, compelling her to dance. Again the dancers run about healing the sick. Two or more theurgists sometimes grab at the same patient simultaneously. The patient often rubs the back of the theurgist during the healing.

The a'kwamosi (maker of the medicine water) stands by the altar keeping time with his plumes, held in each hand and moved simultaneously up and down. An aged man, much crippled with rheumatism, who comes late in the evening, receives treatment from many of the theurgists, who seem especially interested in his case. The largest number of women observed on the floor at any one time is seven, and these, with the number of men crowding the floor, form a curious living kaleidoscope. The dance closes shortly before midnight. The a'kwamosi dips his plumes into the medicine-water and places the quill ends at the lips of the Sia guests.

The final ceremony of sprinkling the altar with sacred meal and administration of the sacred water to each member is similar to that of the preceding night.

The third night was similar to the first except that there was no ritual over the initiates, and the floor was frequently cleared to allow unusually expert healers to perform alone. These solo treatments usually involved some distinctive dance form, many remarkably graceful and picturesque. A further difference was the use of eagle feathers carried in the left hand as a supplement to the sucking operations. The theurgist approached the patient with the plume pointed at the supposed site of the disease and agitated with a suave fluttering motion, somewhat suggestive of the flight of a humming bird. Dozens of these plumes in motion produced a charming effect.

The fourth and final night found the walls of the room decorated with paintings of the Beast Gods. The women's costumes remained the same; but the limbs and bodies of the men were entirely covered with red hematite. The sanctification rituals were repeated as on the preceding nights. The healing of the patients was continued as on the first two nights, except that by clever sleight of hand tricks actual articles seemed to be drawn from the bodies of the patients after the sucking had provided a point of egress for the materials. The observer, claiming to be suffering from a headache, was treated by several theurgists who pretended to extract from her forehead matter "shot" in by the witches. Although it was impossible for her to detect how it was done the healers seemed to withdraw from her forehead several large pebbles and yards of yarn. The general treatment was interrupted several times to allow guest theurgists from other Mystery Medicine Fraternities to carry out their own form of therapeutics; and also to welcome the initiates with an introductory ritual. Later they tried their hand at the healing art of their fraternity. There were also intermissions during which the audience watched dances performed by one, two or three of their numbers. The recorder states that several of them were as beautiful as any she had ever seen in a ballet on the civilized stage. With the usual closing ceremonies the four-day sequence ended about seven the next morning.

### CEREMONIES FOR THE RENEWAL OF THE MEDICINE-MAN'S SUPERNATURAL POWERS

A certain type of medicine ceremony was conducted by some tribes for the purpose of renewing the medicine-men's powers through an intimate communion with the supernatural agents who deputed such powers. As a side issue they usually entailed public performances to impress the people with the magical skill of the shamans. In some tribes these particular ceremonies were purported to be a prophylactic against disease and in a few, as the one described later, healing was done, but was a minor incidental of the chief purpose of the ceremony.

The following is the annual autumn ceremony of the oldest Pawnee medical society, that of the Pumpkin Vine Village. On the return from the fall hunt the chief medicine-men sent out a call to the society members to assemble in the medicine lodge. When they had gathered they were notified to prepare for the ceremony by a four-day fast. This was in accordance with the saga of the hero-god founder of the society; and in this and the other events of the ceremony the myth of origin is closely followed. All the members then scattered into the waste places, each alone and taking with him only his medicine bag. And four days were spent in solitary fasting and prayer. On the morning of the fifth day they bathed and returned to the lodge.

The rest of that day was spent, to the frequent accompaniment of prayers of supplication to the gods, in gathering material for the construction of the booths and figures which were to be set up in the lodge. The next morning the image of the water-monster was made. This was a serpent some 60 ft. long encircling the inner wall of the lodge, and with a wide open mouth large enough to admit the body of a man. The figure of the old woman who was a feature of the legend, and of the turtle were made the next day and the loon skin altar was set up then. As soon as these were all complete and in their traditional places a ceremony was conducted by which each medicine-man received a rejuvenation of his powers from one or the other of the symbolic figures.

The following day, the eighth, a cedar tree was cut and set up inside the entrance of the lodge. Half the society went on the search for the tree. When a suitable one was found, the cutting party surrounded it, offered a sacrifice of blankets amid certain prayers and dances, and felled it. As it fell they mesmerized one another and performed sleight of hand tricks. As they approached the village with the tree they were met by the balance of the society who tried to drive them back by hypnotism. In this they never succeeded as the fir tree lent the bearers a power to overcome the adversaries and triumphantly plant the tree within the lodge. That evening the images of the heavenly beings and the Morning Star were made and the latter raised on a pole above the lodge as the morning star rose.

At sunrise the next morning the medicine-men dressed, each to represent his guardian earth spirit (usually animal) and danced four times, first around the inside and then the outside of the lodge, imitating the gestures and cries of the gods they represented and displaying their skill in leger-demain. A feast was held inside the lodge. After this they danced in a procession to visit the families which owned sacred bundles, and danced in the lodge of each. On their return, certain members were sent out to locate those in the village who might be ill. When these returned, others were sent out to treat the ailing.

During all these and the further ceremonies, certain members called "Kitscoa" acted as clowns. They wore masks made of corn husks, raw hide, wood and feathers; dressed grotesquely and daubed their bodies with colored mud. They performed strange antics, to amuse the people, in particular burlesquing the actions of the serious performers.

The following day the medicine-men again donned their ceremonial apparel and danced and performed their tricks outside the lodge. This was done four times during the day. That night a great fire was built inside the lodge and all the members of the village were invited in to witness an exhibition of the members' skill in magic. This was repeated nightly for a month. It was during this time that candidates were taught the mysteries.

At the end of the month the booths and images were carried to a shallow place in the river and set up in the same relative position they held in the lodge, and they were gradually destroyed by the running water. After the ceremony of disposal, the chief medicine-men returned to the lodge and following a set ritual, dismantled the altar and wrapped the parts in a bundle, which remained a sacred relic until opened the following fall. The floor was then sprinkled with water to free it from the powers that had been summoned there during the ceremony. A smoke offering to the animal gods terminated this protracted rite.

Most of the other tribes in which the medicine-men were organized in societies had similar restorative ceremonies, the rituals varying to meet the myth of origin of the individual society.

The various ceremonies described and referred to here were obviously component and intimate parts of the Indians' practice of medicine and must not be confused with the other so-called Medicine Dances or ceremonies. This other class were more numerous and were cultural, religious and social. Such were the Hako, Dog Dance, Bull Dance, Ghost Dance, etc. Another large group were connected with functions of the clan or social group systems as the Medicine Dances of the Menomini, Poncha, Dakota, etc. The confusion arises because any manifestation of the occult was called "medicine."

FORMALIZED CEREMONIES FOR THERAPEUTIC PURPOSES*

Navajo

    Shooting Arrow Chants
    Devil Chasing Chant
    Night Chant
    Mountain Chant

Pawnee

    Twenty-day Ceremony
    Doctor Dance
    Bear Society Ceremony
    Buffalo Doctors' Ceremony
    Deer Society Dance
    Blood Doctors' Ceremony
    Iruska Society Ceremony
    One Horn Society Ceremony

* There were probably among other tribes many more such ceremonies, this list represents all about which clear descriptions could be found. Many so called "Medicine Dances" had no therapeutic object, being social, religious or military in character.

Zuni Ceremonies
   Shiwannakwe Fraternity
   Newekwe Fraternity
   Uhuhukwee Fraternity
   Holokwe Fraternity
   Shumaakwe Fraternity
   Make Sannakwe Fraternity
   Peshasilokwe Fraternity
   Koskikwe Fraternity

Shohomish
   Shaker Ceremony

Menomini
   Mide Wiwin Grand Medical Ceremony.

Cheyenne
   Maussam Ceremony

# CHAPTER IX

## CONCLUSIONS

The practice of medicine among the American Indians should only be evaluated by a comparison with the medical practices of other civilizations at the same stage of development. Except for a relatively small group of the Southwest who had come under the influence of the advanced Mexican culture, the great body of the American Indians were living in the Stone Age in a hunting culture, where agriculture was present in rudimentary form. This was scarcely altered by their use of metal and guns after contact with the whites, as it did not introduce a true iron culture. They were true Stone Age men as late as 1870. But their medical practices were far in advance of the Stone Age, being comparable to that of Chaldeans, Assyrians, Hebrews, and early Greeks, and with that of an isolated period in the Middle Ages in Europe. The common basis of all these groups was a demonological theory of disease.

Even as compared with their contemporary whites, they were not entirely to be scorned. Their treatment of wounds, fractures, and empyema was equal to or better than that of the white physicians of the 18th century. Their handling of the retained placenta anticipated Credé by a century. They were considerably behind, however, in the understanding of internal medicine and had no knowledge of contagious diseases.

When the medical practices of their non-medical white contemporaries are considered, the Indian appears at a still greater advantage. A suggestion of the therapeutics of the white of the rural Middle West as late as 1890 is illuminating in this respect. Children of stunted growth were passed through holes in trees. Babies were weaned at certain signs of the zodiac. The "madstone," a cartilage from the heart of the deer, was used as an antidote for hydrophobia. Mysterious charms, incantations and gibberish were recited to control hemorrhage. A pan of water was placed under the bed to prevent night sweats. "Nanny tea," made of goats' dung was given in eruptive fevers, etc. Nor do we have to go back further than the present year to note Amerind practices among our modern urban civilization. Witness our host of Faith Healers, and the recent excitement over the grave of a priest in Melrose, Mass. And recently, the Belmont Park authorities paid $10,000 to a man who promised to prevent rainfall during the racing week.

The Indian added 59 drugs to our modern pharmacopeia, including cascara sagrada, lobelia, puccoon, cohorh, pipsissewa and dockmackie. And to certain famous medicine-men who ministered to the pioneer whites, the whites of that generation owed a debt of gratitude. Such were Joe Pye, Sabbatus and Molly Orcutt in New England, Tonneraouanont among the Hurons and the old Sioux, Baptiste. The latter was a shaman of a tribe at the Winnebago agency at a time when there were no white physicians within several hundred miles. When his tribe was moved to a more western reserve he was kept at the Winnebago agency. The government built Baptiste a house and maintained him, and for years he treated the

Indian and white alike, finally dying respected and admired by both races.

In short, we may conclude that the medical practices of the American Indian, living in the practical equivalent of our Stone Age, were marked by sincerity, confidence and picturesqueness and were in many respects effective. Much of their work had a rational basis and at a few points they were in advance of the civilized practice of their day and age.

# BIBLIOGRAPHY

ANDREWS, E. *Chicago Med. Exam.*, 10: 599, 1869.
ANDROS, F. *J. A. M. A.*, 1: 116, 1883.
ANDROS, F. *Lancet*, 1: 611, 1904.
BENEDICT, A. L. *Med. Age*, 19: 767, 1901.
BISSELL, G. P. *Cal. M. J.*, 10: 227, 1889.
BLAIR, E. H. Indian Tribes of the Upper Mississippi and Region of the Great Lakes. Arthur H. Clark Co., 1912.
BROOKS, H. *Bull. N. York Acad. Med.*, 5: 509, 1929.
BUCHANAN, C. M. *St. Louis Cour. Med.*, 21: 277, 355, 1899.
CARR, L. *Proc. Am. Antiqu. Soc.*, n.s. 13: 448, 1901.
CATLIN, G. North American Indians. Phila. Hazard, 1857.
CHAMBERLAIN, A. F. *Proc. Am. Antiqu. Soc.* n.s. 16: 91, 1905.
CONYNGHAM, E. F. *J. A. M. A.*, 41: 323, 1905.
COOLIDGE, D. and M. R. The Navajo Indians. Boston, Houghton Mifflin, 1930.
CURRIER, A. F. *Trans. Am. Gynec. Soc.*, 16: 264, 1891.
DARLING, WINDWE, W. *Boston M. & S. J.*, 34: 9, 1846.
DENIG, E. T. *St. Louis M. & S. J.*, 13: 312, 1855.
DORSAY, G. *Mem. Am. Folklore Soc.*, 8: 1904.
DOWLER, B. *New Orleans M. & S. J.*, 14: 335, 1857.
ENGELMANN, G. *J. Am. J. Obst.*, 14: 303; 602; 828; 1881; 15: 601, 1882.
FERGUSSON, ERNA. Dancing Gods. N. Y., Knopf, 1931.
FLETCHER, A. C. Part II, 22nd Ann. Report, Bur. Am. Ethnol., Smithson. Inst., 1900–1901 (1904).
GIBBS, G. Part II, U. S. Geographical and Geological Survey of the Rocky Mountain Region. Washington, D. C., 1877.
GILMORE, M. R. 33rd Ann. Report Bur. Am. Ethnol., Smithson. Inst., 1911–1912 (1919) p. 45.
GORTON, D. A. Medical History. N. Y., Putnam, 1910, 2: 249.
GRINNELL, F. *Cincin. Lancet. & Obs.*, n.s. 17: 145, 1874.
GRINNELL, G. B. Pawnee Hero Stories and Folk Tales. N. Y., Scribners, 1889.
The Cheyenne Indians. New Haven, Yale Univ. Press, 1924.
The Fighting Cheyennes. N. Y., Scribners, 1915.
HOLDER, A. B. *Am. J. Obst.*, 25: 752, 1892; 26: 41, 1892.

HOFFMAN, W. J. *Med. & Surg. Rep.*, 40: 157, 1879.
HRDLICKA, A. *Washington Med. Ann.*, 5: 372, 1905.
   *Bull. No. 34, Bur. Am. Ethnol. Smithson. Inst.* 1906–1907.
IRA, G. W. *Western Med. Rev.*, 1: 89, 1896.
JENNER, E F. L. *Pharmaceutical Era*, 25: 144, 1901.
JOSELYN, J., New England's Rarities. Boston, Wm. Veazie, 1865.
KENNARD, T. *St. Louis M. & S. J.*, 16: 389, 1858.
KING, J. E. *Southern Cal. Practitioner*, 12, 41: 1887.
KUYKENDALL, G. B. *Med. & Surg. Rep.*, 33: 181, 1875.
LINTON, R. Field Mus. Natural History, Leaflet 8, 1923.
LOSKIEL, G. H. History of the Mission of the United Brethren among the North American Indians. Trans. by C. I. LaTrobe, London, 1794.
LYND, R. S. and H. M. Middletown. Boston, Houghton, Mifflin, 1929.
M'CLENACHEN, H. H. *Med. & Surg. Rep.*, 44: 338, 1881.
MINER, W. H. The American Indians North of Mexico. Cambridge University Press, 1917.
OETTEKING, B. Indian Notes, Mus. Am. Indian, Heye Foundation N. Y., VII. 1: 52, 1930.
PARKER, A. C. Archaeological Rep. Ontario Prov. Mus., 1928.
POWERS, S. U. S. Geographical and Geological Survey of the Rocky Mountain Region. Washington, D. C., 1877, vol. 3.
PRENTISS, D., and MORGAN F. P. *Therapeutic Gaz.*, w. s. 19, 11: 577, 1895.
ROBBINS, W. W. *Bull. No. 55 Bur. Am. Ethnol. Smithson. Inst.*, 1916.
RUSH, B. Medical Inquiries and Observations., Phila., 1805, 1: 3.
SAFFORD, W. E. *Ann. Rep. Smithson. Inst.*, 1916, p. 387.
SCHOOLCRAFT, H. Thirty Years with the Indian Tribes. Lippincott, Grambo Co., 1851.
SKINNER, A. Indian Notes and Monographs, IV, 1920, Mus. of Am. Indian, Heye Foundation, N. Y.
SMITH, E. A. *2nd. Ann. Rep., Bur. Am. Ethnol. Smithson. Inst.* 1880–81 (1883), p. 47.
STEVENSON, M. C. *23rd. Ann. Rep., Bur. Am. Ethnol. Smithson. Inst.* 1901–1902 (1904).
   *30th. Ann. Rep., Bu. Am. Ethnol. Smithson. Inst.* 1908–1909 (1915).
STRATTON, T. *Edinburgh M. & S. J.*, 81: 269, 1894.

SWANTON, J. R. 42nd, Ann. Rep. Bur. Am. Ethnol. Smithson. Inst. p. 171, 1924–25 (1928).
  44th. Ann. Rep. Bur. Am. Ethnol. Smithson. Inst. p. 171, 1926–27 (1929).
TONER, J. M. Virg. M. Monthly, 4: 334, 1877.
WHITEBREAD, C. Proc. U. S. Nat. Mus., 67: Art. 10, 1923.
WILLIAMSON, T. S. Northwest M. & S. J., 55: 410, 1873–4.
WILSON, N. W. Buffalo M. J., n.s. 41: 740, 1901–2.
WISSLER, C. North American Indians of the Plains. N. Y., Am. Mus. Nat. Hist., 1927.
WOODRUFF, C. Med. Rec., 39: 104, 1891.

FIG. 17. Map showing location of

Indian tribes referred to in this book.

# INDEX OF PERSONAL NAMES

# INDEX OF SUBJECTS

CPSIA information can be obtained
at www.ICGtesting.com
Printed in the USA
BVHW052232221222
654900BV00007B/54